# Culinary Arts Institute

# MEXICAN COOKBOOK

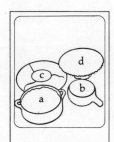

*Featured in cover photo:*
a. **Chicken Tablecloth Stainer, 42**
b. **Corn Soup I, 58**
c. **Guacamole II, 65**
d. **Coconut Flan, 79**

# MEXICAN COOKBOOK

MEXICAN COOKBOOK

**The Culinary Arts Institute Staff:**
Helen Geist: Director
Sherrill Corley and Margot Newsom: Editors
Edward Finnegan: Executive Editor • Charles Bozett: Art Director
Ethel La Roche: Editorial Assistant • Ivanka Simatic: Recipe Tester
Malinda Miller: Copy Editor • Laurel DiGangi: Art Assembly

Book designed and coordinated by Charles Bozett and John Mahalek

Illustrations by Ramon Orellana

Cover photo: Bob Scott Studios     Inside photos: Zdenek Pivecka

Adventures in Cooking SERIES

# Culinary Arts Institute
1727 South Indiana Avenue, Chicago, Illinois 60616

# CONTENTS

# INTRODUCTION

Modern Mexican cooking is as rich in history as it is in taste. If you eat a taco covered with tangy tomato sauce, or drink a cup of hot chocolate, you travel back in time over four hundred years to enjoy some of the delicacies of Montezuma, Emperor of the Aztecs. Eat a paella, and you dine with Spanish kings!

When, in the early 1500's, the Spanish Conquistadores, led by Cortés, invaded Mexico and encountered the Aztec civilization, they were as surprised to find many new foods and cookery methods as they were to see the pyramids. Montezuma, it seems, had as much interest in culinary art as he had in science; the culinary advancement of the ancient Aztecs equaled their remarkable achievements in the fields of mathematics, astronomy, and engineering. Perhaps we do not realize today how many foods that are now staples of the world diet were unknown in Europe until they were introduced from the Americas in the early sixteenth century.

The most important of these foods was corn. The Indians of tropical middle America first cultivated wild corn at least seven thousand years ago. The Spanish quickly accepted corn because it returned a yield ten times that of any grain then grown in the Old World.

Surprisingly, tomatoes were also unknown in Europe, although we tend to think of them as coming from Italy. Turkeys, too, provided a new taste treat for the Conquistadores. Other new and unusual foods, which we take for granted today, included sweet potatoes, peanuts, beans, squash, pumpkins, chilies, cocoa, vanilla, and avocados. Cortés and his men also learned of such tropical fruits as pineapples, coconuts, mangos, and melons.

Just as the Spaniards returned home with new foods, they also brought many from their homeland to introduce to the New World. Most important of these were domestic animals—cattle, pigs, sheep, and goats. These permitted the

addition of meat and dairy products to a diet which had previously included little animal protein (turkeys apparently had been the main source) and also provided a more plentiful source of fats, primarily lard. The Indians learned how to cook with lard, and it became the basic cooking fat of Mexico. In return, they taught the Spaniards how to barbecue their meat products, enhancing them with spicy sauces. With the addition of rice and wine, the two great culinary traditions merged to become one—Mexican.

The Spaniards also introduced their cooking techniques, which blended with the methods developed by the Indians to produce many unusual dishes. Most of these more elaborate foods were prepared for the enjoyment of government or military officials; the lower classes probably existed on simpler fare. During the brief reign of Maximilian and Carlotta in the mid-1800's, French, Austrian, and Italian dishes were served to the court, and some of these dishes were absorbed into the Mexican cuisine. In more recent years the North American influence has been felt, though perhaps more in restaurant fare than in the Mexican home kitchen.

Even with all these outside influences, Mexican cooking today bears a great similarity to that of the Aztecs. Corn (as used in the ever-present tortillas, tacos, and tamales), beans, and chilies continue to be the most important foods in Mexican cooking, as they have been for hundreds of years. These foods are so basic that seldom is a meal put on the table without all three in some form. A myriad of fruits and vegetables, meats, fish, and poultry are available to vary the theme of Mexican cooking, while corn, beans, and chilies are the theme itself.

Today's menus still include many of the dishes that history tells us were served to Montezuma. Among these are tamales filled with meat, beans, fruit, or nuts; pork or chicken pibil (meat wrapped in corn husks or banana leaves and cooked in a pit); and atole, the beverage made from diluted corn dough sweetened and flavored with chocolate or fruit. Montezuma also enjoyed the chili and tomato mole sauces. But the well-known mole poblano sauce, legend has it, was created by the nuns at the convent of Santa Rosa who unexpectedly received a visit from their archbishop. Having little time to prepare a dinner worthy of such an occasion, the nuns, it is said, added chocolate and everything they could find to their mole sauce, thus creating the famous sauce that is with us today.

## MEXICAN MEALTIMES

The delights of Mexican cuisine are displayed in the traditional five daily meals. Breakfast, *desayuno*, is served quite early at home, usually just coffee with milk and bread or tortillas. In mid to late morning a larger breakfast called *almuerzo* is served. This meal can include eggs, beans, tortillas, chili sauce, and coffee. This is somewhat the reverse of our North American custom of having a big early breakfast plus a mid-morning coffee break.

The main meal of the day, called *comida*, is served in the early to mid-afternoon siesta period, and is generally a family affair. Many businesses and stores close for two to three hours in the afternoon while employees go home for the comida. In Mexico City, and to some extent in Guadalajara, Mexico's second largest city, this custom is gradually changing due to the time involved in transportation to and from business. But the rest of Mexico still follows this custom.

The comida, depending on the occasion, begins with appetizers and is followed by soup. The next course is another soup, the dry soup or *sopa seca*, of pasta, rice, or tortillas. Fish, followed by meat or poultry with a salad and vegetables, makes up the main course. The dessert can be either a sweet or fruit.

In the early evening a light snack meal called *merienda* is served, usually a cup of hot chocolate or coffee with tortillas. The *cena,* or supper, follows any time after 8:00 P.M. If the main meal of the day was the comida, this will be quite light. If it is a special day—perhaps a fiesta day or family birthday—guests may be invited and the meal will be served quite late, even as late as midnight. The cena in a restaurant will never start before 9:00 P.M., and usually much later. Therefore, foreign visitors to Mexican restaurants will find them quite empty until after 10:00 P.M.

For those who lead busy lives and find it difficult to return home for meals, street foodstands abound. Often the stands are mobile, and sometimes may be nothing more than a three-wheeled bicycle which the owner rides from place to place shouting out his menu. Fruits and juices prepared fresh on location, seafoods, tacos and tostadas cooked on the spot, tamales kept hot in a steamer, atole ladled from a huge kettle, and tortas (sandwiches made on crisp-crusted rolls), in addition to the usual candy and soft drinks, are some of the foods sold from such mobile snack bars.

## THE MEXICAN MARKET

Grocery shopping in Mexico is an interesting and colorful experience. Although there is an increasing number of supermarkets springing up throughout the country, most of the food buying is still done in open markets. An open market often is set up around or near the town square in smaller villages, and may be held only one day each week. In large cities there are permanent open markets which aren't really open at all, but are actually a series of booths and stalls under one huge roof. Such a market may cover an area of two city blocks, and sell everything found in a modern department store plus a supermarket. Each stall or *impuesta* is presided over by its proprietor, probably helped by a few family members, and may sell as few as half a dozen different items. The shopper moves from stall to stall, with a shopping basket over her arm, selecting apples, tortillas, beans, meats, nuts, or whatever else she needs. Each food is weighed on a hanging scale, paid for, and put in her basket, usually unwrapped.

### THE MODERN MEXICAN KITCHEN

The modern Mexican kitchen looks much like a typical kitchen in the United States. The old-fashioned clay *comal* for baking tortillas has been replaced by an iron or cast-aluminum griddle, often present as a permanent section of the modern gas or electric range. Instead of a *metate* with its accompanying *metlalpil* for grinding and blending chilies with other ingredients, the modern cook uses an electric blender. Add a tortilla press and a good-sized steamer for tamales to the usual equipment of any U.S. kitchen, and you can prepare any of the recipes in this book.

Whether you are planning a Mexican fiesta (party) with colorful decorations and exciting taste treats for your guests, or you just want to try something new for a snack, you'll find that Mexican dishes are as easy to prepare as they are to eat. So enjoy, and

*Buen Provecho*

# GLOSSARY

**Adobo sauce** (ah-THOUGH-bo)—a dark red sauce made with ancho chilies and tomatoes, used for meats, poultry, and vegetables

**Albóndigas** (al-BONE-thee-gahs)—meatballs, in Mexico almost always using three or four different meats

**Almuerzo** (alm-WHERRR-so)—the large breakfast or brunch, usually served in mid to late morning

**Ancho chilies** (AHN-cho)—mild, sweet chilies, somewhat resembling the green bell pepper, and the most commonly used in Mexican cooking; they are sold fresh when an immature green or mature red, or dried and almost black

**Annatto seeds**—seeds of a tropical tree; also called *achiote* (ah-chee-OH-tay)

**Atole** (ah-TOE-lay)—sweet beverage made with corn masa, milk, and various flavorings

**Buñuelos** (boon-you-EY-los)—wafer-thin, crisp, deep-fried pastries

**Burritos** (boo-RRREE-toes)—tacos made with tortillas of wheat flour

**Campurrado** (kahm-poo-RRRAH-doe)—chocolate atole

**Capirotada** (kah-pee-roe-TAH-thah)—bread pudding with nuts and raisins

**Cena** (SAY-nah)—a festive, late night dinner

**Chihuahua cheese** (chee-WHA-wha)—creamy-colored, moist cheese with mild flavor, a favorite in Mexican dishes, similar to Monterey Jack cheese in the United States

**Chile** (CHEE-lay)—the podlike fruit which is used as the major flavoring in Mexican cooking; usually spelled *chili* in the United States

**Chipotle chili** (chee-POE-lay)—medium-sized, dark red to brown, hot chili with distinctive flavor, usually sold pickled in cans

**Chorizo** (choe-REE-so)—highly seasoned, usually chili-hot, Mexican pork sausage

**Churros** (CHEW-rrroes)—long, stringlike, crisp, deep-fried pastries or snacks

**Cilantro** (see-LAHN-trrow)—leafy green herb, sometimes called Chinese parsley or fresh coriander, with a strong distinctive flavor; often used fresh sprinkled over dishes

**Comal** (coe-MAL)—old-fashioned, clay baking surface, used in Mexico to bake tortillas

**Comida** (coe-ME-thah)—Mexico's dinner, most often served in midafternoon

**Comino** (coe-ME-no)—also called cumin, a commonly used spice in Mexican cooking

**Dehydrated masa flour**—sometimes called instant masa, flour made from dried corn masa dough

**Desayuno** (des-ah-YOU-no)—Mexican early morning breakfast

**Dry soup**—casserole-like dish for which rice, pasta, or tortillas are cooked in seasoned broth until all water is absorbed

**Empanadas** (em-pah-NAH-thahs)—Mexican-style turnovers, filled with meat or sweets

**Enchiladas** (en-chee-LA-thahs)—tortilla-based dish, for which the tortillas are dipped in sauce, lightly fried, then filled and rolled

**Escabeche** (es-cah-VEY-chay)—cooked fish in a pickle, onion, and chili brine

**Flan** (FLAHN)—caramel-topped baked custard

**Garbanzos** (garrr-VAHN-soes)—chickpeas

**Gazpacho** (gahs-PAH-choe)—cold soup of fresh raw vegetables

**Guacamole** (gwah-cah-MOE-lay)—cold sauce of chopped avocados

**Instant masa**—*see* **Dehydrated masa flour**

**Jalapeño chili** (hah-la-PEN-yo)—very hot, small green chilies, often sold canned

**Jamaica** (hah-MAH-i-cah)—sweet drink made by soaking dried jamaica flowers in water

**Jícama** (HE-cah-mah)—large, gray-brown, crisp-textured root vegetable, most often eaten raw

**Kilogram**—metric weight used for purchasing food in Mexico (as well as much of the rest of the world); equivalent to approximately 2.2 lbs.

**Lomo** (LOE-mo)—boneless pork loin

**Maguey** (mah-GOO-ey)—succulent plant with

long, pointed, blue-gray leaves, also called agave or century plant; tequila is made from maguey

**Masa, masa dough** (MAH-sah)—dough prepared from lime-treated corn kernels, from which tortillas are made

**Masa harina** (MAH-sah are-EEN-ah)—*see* **Dehydrated masa flour**

**Metate** (may-TAH-tay)—rough stone mortar used in Mexican kitchens for grinding and blending chilies, tomatoes, etc. for various sauces

**Metlalpil** (may-tal-PEEL)—rough stone pestle used with the metate

**Merienda** (meh-ree-EN-thah)—the light supper served in early evening in Mexican homes

**Mexican chocolate** (choe-coe-LAH-tay)—cakes of sweetened chocolate, blended with cinnamon and sometimes almonds, for preparing hot chocolate beverage

**Mole** (MOE-lay)—chili-based sauce used in Mexican cooking; most familiar is the mole poblano (MOE-lay poe-BLAH-no), which uses unsweetened chocolate

**Molinello** (moe-lee-NELL-yo)—a wooden beater for hot chocolate

**Monterey Jack cheese**—creamy-colored, mild-flavored cheese sold in the United States; similar to Chihuahua cheese

**Nixtamal** (knees-tah-MAL)—dried corn which has been soaked in lime water before it is ground into masa

**Pasilla chili** (pah-SEAL-ya)—very dark red chili, quite hot

**Pasta** (PAH-stah)—macaroni, spaghetti, noodles, and other similar products, whatever their shape, made from a dough of durum wheat

**Pepitas** (pay-PEE-tahs)—pumpkin seeds

**Pibil** (pee-BEEL)—a word derived from the Mayan word "pib" meaning barbecue pit, and applied to Mexican barbecued meats cooked in a pit

**Picadillo** (pee-cah-DILL-yo)—meat filling made with shredded, cooked meat plus vegetables and/or fruits and seasonings

**Picante** (pee-CAHN-tay)—chili-hot

**Pipián** (pee-pee-AHN)—sauce made with sesame and/or pumpkin seeds

**Polvorones** (poll-vor-OH-nez)—cookies rolled in confectioners' sugar or sugar-cinnamon mixture; literally "dusted ones"

**Pomegranate** (poe-may-grah-NAH-tay)—red tropical fruit with large red juicy seeds which are often used in salads

**Pozole** (poe-SEW-lay)—rich pork stew native to the Mexican state of Jalisco

**Pulque** (POOL-kay)—beverage made from the fermented sap of one variety of the maguey plant

**Quesadilla** (kay-sah-DILL-ya)—a fried cheese taco

**Refried beans**—mashed, cooked dried beans which have been refried in lard and seasoned for eating

**Refritos** (rrray-FREE-toes)—*see* **Refried beans**

**Rompope** (rrrome-POE-pay)—Mexican beverage similar to eggnog

**Salsa casera** (SAL-sah cah-SEH-rah)—slightly picante sauce of tomatoes and chilies, frequently sold canned for table use

**Salsa verde Mexicana** (SAL-sah VERRR-day may-he-CAH-nah)—slightly picante green sauce made with the Mexican green tomato (tomatillo)

**Sangría** (san-GREE-ah) fruit-flavored red wine

**Seviche** (say-VEE-chay)—pickled raw fish appetizer (also spelled *ceviche*)

**Steamer**—two-part kettle, rather like a double boiler, used for cooking tamales; top section has holes in the bottom to permit steam to circulate through foods placed in it

**Taco** (TAH-co)—tortilla, filled with meat, cheese, beans, etc., rolled and served hot, or deep-fat-fried until crisp

**Tamale** (tah-MAH-lay)—moist corn masa dough enclosing spicy filling of meat, poultry, etc., and wrapped in corn husks for cooking

**Tequila** (tay-KEE-lah)—clear, distilled alcoholic beverage made from the maguey plant

**Tomatillo** (toe-mah-TILL-yo)—Mexican green tomato; a small, olive-green fruit with firm flesh, enclosed in a papery husk; used to make salsa verde and other Mexican dishes

**Tortilla** (torrr-TILL-yah)—very thin, baked, breadlike patty made from corn masa

**Tortillería** (torrr-till-yer-EE-ah)—store devoted to the preparation and selling of tortillas

**Tostadas** (toes-TAH-dahs)—crisp fried tortillas, covered with various fillings and eaten like an open-face sandwich

**Zucchini**—small, mild-flavored squash, usually shaped somewhat like a cucumber

# CORN DISHES

## TORTILLAS

### TORTILLA MAKING AND DISHES MADE WITH TORTILLAS

Most of the corn consumed in Mexico is eaten as tortillas. Though tortillas are often referred to as the national bread of Mexico, they really are much more than this. Besides being the breadlike accompaniment to meals, and the "wrapper" of tacos and enchiladas, tortillas also appear as the "pasta" of many casserole-type dishes and soups.

The ancient Indian people of Mexico made their tortillas from corn kernels dried on the ears in the fields. These kernels (of white corn, incidentally, not the more frequently used yellow corn of the northern United States) were soaked in lime water until the skins could be rubbed off easily. The wet corn, *nixtamal*, was then ground by hand on a flat stone mortar, *metate*, with a stone pestle, *metlalpil*, until fine enough to form a fairly stiff dough called *masa*. This masa was then patted between the palms of the hands into very thin patty shapes (tortillas) and finally baked on a flat clay baking *comal* over an open fire for about two minutes per side. This same process is followed today to produce tortillas, sometimes with the same type of hand equipment (still sold in big markets in Mexico), but more commonly by machine.

Many Mexican cooks today still make their own tortillas. They may buy packaged *masa harina* (dehydrated masa flour) to which they simply add water. But more commonly, the cook will purchase fresh, ready-made masa. This moist dough is sold by the kilogram in most Mexican markets. The masa is formed into small balls and patted or pressed (with a tortilla press) into thin patties and baked on a griddle.

In cities and large towns in Mexico, the housewife who has neither the time nor the inclination to make her own tortillas may purchase them freshly made and still warm at a local tortillería. In these little specialty shops the national bread is turned out as a finished product on a machine like those which make pizza dough in U.S. pizzerias. The customers line up at midday, each carrying a napkin-lined basket or plastic container in which to carry home the tortillas.

In areas of the United States which have sizeable Mexican populations, not only are the ingredients for tortillas available, but you'll probably find tortillerías and Mexican grocery stores turning out machine-made tortillas. In other areas, many big supermarkets carry tortillas already baked, frozen, or canned in the soft form; or as the crisp-baked tortillas usually formed into a fold-over shape ready to be filled as tacos. In some supermarkets, packaged masa harina is also available, so you too can make your own fresh-baked tortillas.

# Corn Tortillas

1 teaspoon salt
2 cups dehydrated masa flour
    (masa harina)
1⅓ cups hot water

1. Stir salt into masa flour. Add water and stir until all flour is moistened and dough sticks together. Add a little more water if necessary; dough should be soft, but not sticky.
2. Break off pieces of dough about the size of a large egg, form into balls, and flatten slightly. Press with a tortilla press (or roll with rolling pin) between two sheets of waxed paper to 6-inch rounds.
3. Bake on a preheated ungreased griddle, about 2 minutes per side; tortillas are ready to be turned when edges begin to curl. Stack hot baked tortillas in a towel-lined bowl. Serve hot.

*12 tortillas*

*Note:* Unused tortillas may be wrapped in moisture-proof wrap and stored in the refrigerator. To reheat, simply dampen slightly and warm on a medium-hot griddle, turning several times. Immediately wrap in towel to retain heat until served. Do not let them dry out.

In the northern part of Mexico, where a good deal of wheat is grown, tortillas are often made with wheat flour. These are more delicate than corn masa tortillas, and have a very different flavor and texture. They are easy to make, the method being similar to that used in the United States to make pastry and biscuits. Usually wheat flour tortillas are made in 7-inch rounds. However, in the northern Mexican state of Sonora the women make a specialty of huge wheat flour tortillas, patting and pulling them by hand to as much as two feet in diameter. If you have a large griddle, you too can make griddle-sized tortillas, shaping with a rolling pin, then rolling the huge tortillas loosely onto your rolling pin and unrolling onto the griddle for baking.

# Wheat Flour Tortillas

2 cups all-purpose flour
1 teaspoon salt
1 teaspoon baking powder
¼ cup lard or shortening
½ to ¾ cup cold water

1. Stir flour with salt and baking powder in bowl. Cut in lard until pieces are the size of small peas. Sprinkle water on top and mix lightly until all dry ingredients are moistened, adding only enough water to make a soft dough.
2. Turn out on a lightly floured surface or pastry canvas and knead gently, about 30 seconds. Divide into 12 equal balls; cover with a towel or waxed paper and let stand about 15 minutes. Roll each ball to a 7-inch round.
3. Bake on an ungreased griddle until lightly browned, turning once; use 2 to 3 minutes total baking time.

*12 tortillas*

## HOW TO HANDLE READY-MADE TORTILLAS

*Freshly made purchased tortillas:* If you are fortunate enough to live near a Mexican grocery or tortillería where you can obtain freshly made tortillas, you will still probably need to reheat them before serving. If the tortillas are still warm when you purchase them, and you do not plan to serve them immediately, it is a good idea to separate them until they have cooled, then stack and rewrap in moisture-proof wrap until mealtime. When ready to serve, if planning to serve soft tortillas, simply heat them on a medium-hot griddle about 30 seconds, then wrap in a towel. If your recipe requires crisp-fried tortillas, it is necessary to reheat before frying.

*Canned or frozen packaged tortillas:* Canned tortillas are usually packaged with paper between them to prevent sticking. Simply peel off paper and reheat about 30 seconds on a medium-hot griddle, or fry as needed. Frozen tortillas should be thawed before using: lay in a single layer on absorbent paper and let stand about 5 minutes to thaw. Then reheat or fry as needed.

## TACOS

Most North Americans think of tacos as crisp-fried tortillas, folded in half and filled with ground beef or chicken. But in Mexico, tacos are the most varied of all foods. Often they are simply soft tortillas wrapped or folded around a single filling. Frequently the diner may make his own taco of this type from the various foods served in a meal, piling meat, refried beans, and vegetables into soft tortillas, rolling them up and downing them finger-style. Or, soft tortillas may be filled with meat, cheese, beans or other vegetables, even potatoes, rolled or folded to enclose the filling, then fried until crisp in hot lard or oil. Usually tacos are served with an assortment of accompaniments to spoon over the top or add to the filling: shredded lettuce or cabbage, chopped onion, sliced radishes, and always the ever-present sauce which may vary from mild to very hot.

### HOW TO MAKE TACOS

*Tacos with soft tortillas:* Make fresh tortillas or heat purchased soft tortillas on medium-hot ungreased griddle, turning several times. Immediately place in towel-lined bowl and wrap to keep hot. To prepare tacos, simply spoon about 2 tablespoons of chosen filling into center of hot tortilla and fold or roll up to enclose the filling. Offer an assortment of toppings such as shredded cheese, chopped onion, chopped fresh tomatoes, shredded lettuce or cabbage, etc. Diners may either open tacos, put toppings inside, then reroll and eat with their fingers, or sprinkle toppings over filled tacos and eat with a fork.

*Tacos made with crisp-fried folded tortillas:* Fry soft tortillas in hot oil until limp. Fold in half and hold in slightly open position with tongs; continue to fry until crisp, turning to fry on both sides. Remove to absorbent paper and drain well. Fill by spooning filling carefully into "pocket" of tortillas. These tacos are usually eaten with the fingers, but may also be placed on a plate, sprinkled with toppings, and eaten with a fork.

*Tacos of rolled crisp-fried tortillas:* Place chosen filling on one side of soft tortilla. Roll up to completely enclose filling. Fry in hot oil until crisp, starting with open flap on underside, then turning to fry top and sides. These tacos make neat finger-food, but as with their cousins (described above) may also be placed on a plate, topped with vegetables and sauce, and eaten with a fork.

Following are several suggestions for some of the most popular taco fillings. But you may have other favorites. And in Mexico the variety of taco fillings is almost endless, so use your imagination.

## Ground Beef Filling

*This filling may be used alone, but is particularly good sprinkled with shredded mild Cheddar cheese.*

1½ **pounds ground beef**
¼ **cup chopped onion**
1 **clove garlic, minced**
1 **teaspoon salt**
¼ **teaspoon pepper**
1 **teaspoon chili powder**
½ **teaspoon cumin (optional)**
1 **cup canned tomato sauce**

1. Crumble beef into skillet and brown well; if beef is very fat, pour off excess fat.
2. Add onion and garlic and cook about 5 minutes until onion is soft, stirring frequently.
3. Stir in dry seasonings, then tomato sauce. Continue cooking about 15 minutes longer.

*About 3 cups filling*

## Beef-Onion Filling

3 **tablespoons lard**
1 **cup finely chopped onion**
1 **clove garlic, minced**
1 **pound ground beef**
1 **teaspoon salt**
2 **teaspoons chili powder**
  **Pinch ground cumin (comino)**

Heat lard in a large, heavy skillet. Add onion and garlic and cook until tender. Add beef and seasonings; mix well. Cook until meat is lightly browned.

*About 2½ cups filling*

## Chicken Filling

2 **cups diced cooked chicken**
1 **cup Guacamole I (page 65), or 1**
  **fresh avocado**
1 **large fresh tomato, peeled, cored,**
  **and chopped**

1. Combine chicken with guacamole; or, if using fresh avocado, peel and slice avocado into thin strips.
2. To assemble tacos, spoon chicken onto soft tortillas (top with avocado slices, if using fresh avocado). Spoon on a little chopped tomato and close tacos.

The pottery tree-of-life is background for staple ingredients used in Mexican cooking, such as cornmeal, beans, and chilies.

Picadillo is a name given to a wide variety of cooked meat fillings which can be used for either tacos or tamales. Literally the name means "meat and vegetable hash" or "minced meat." The meat is seldom ground, unless the cook is very modern; rather the whole cut of meat is boiled until tender, then pulled apart or shredded into small strips. The other ingredients are then mixed with the meat and the filling is seasoned to taste. Some versions call for vegetables, others for fruits and nuts. Here are two recipes, one for each type.

# Picadillo I

1½ pounds beef (chuck or pot roast may be used)
    Water
¾ cup chopped onion
1 clove garlic, minced
¼ cup cooking oil
1 cup chili sauce
1 cup cooked peas and diced carrots
½ cup beef broth (from cooked meat)
1 teaspoon salt
¼ teaspoon pepper
¼ teaspoon ginger
1 bay leaf, crumbled
1 or more chopped canned jalapeño chilies

1. Cook meat in water to cover until tender (1 to 3 hours, depending upon cut of meat chosen); add more water during cooking if necessary to prevent drying out. Pour off and reserve beef broth.
2. Shred the meat by pulling it apart into small strips.
3. Sauté the onion and garlic in hot oil until onion is soft; add to the meat. Add remaining ingredients and stir until evenly mixed.

*About 3 cups filling*

# Picadillo II

1 pound coarsely chopped beef
1 pound coarsely chopped pork
1 cup chopped onion
1 clove garlic, minced
1 cup chopped raw apple
1½ cups chopped tomatoes (fresh peeled tomatoes or canned tomatoes, drained, may be used)
½ cup raisins
1 or more chopped canned jalapeño chilies
1½ teaspoons salt
¼ teaspoon pepper
⅛ teaspoon cinnamon
⅛ teaspoon cloves
½ cup chopped almonds

1. Cook beef and pork together in large skillet until well browned. Add onion and garlic and cook until onion is soft. Add remaining ingredients, except almonds, and simmer 15 to 20 minutes longer until flavors are well blended and filling is slightly thickened.
2. Stir in almonds.

*About 4½ cups filling*

The colors of the Mexican flag—green, white, and red—are shown in this tray of taco fillings. How to make tacos is on page 15.

# Grilled Meat Filling

1½ pounds thinly sliced beef steak
(cubed steaks may be used if
no more than ¼ inch thick)
Salt and pepper
Oil for frying

1. Sprinkle meat with salt and pepper and rub in slightly.
2. Pour oil into heavy skillet to just cover bottom; heat until sizzling. Quickly fry steaks, turning once; allow about 5 minutes total cooking time.
3. Remove steaks to a heated platter or cutting board and immediately slice into ½-inch squares. Serve at once with **hot soft tortillas** and Fresh Tomato Sauce (page 20).

# Chorizo Filling

*Chorizo is spicy Mexican sausage which is frequently used as filling for tacos, topping for tostadas, in combination with eggs, or in various soups and casserole dishes. It is popular as a taco filling combined with cubed cooked potatoes. You may be able to purchase chorizo in a Mexican specialty store. If not, here is a simple recipe for making your own.*

1 pound ground lean pork
½ cup chopped onion
1 clove garlic, minced
2 tablespoons chili powder
1 teaspoon salt
1 teaspoon oregano
½ teaspoon cumin (comino)
¼ cup vinegar

1. Combine all ingredients and let stand several hours, or overnight, in refrigerator.
2. To use as a filling, fry in skillet until well browned, stirring until crumbled.
3. Serve in tacos, combined with cubed cooked potatoes, refried beans, and/or guacamole.

*About 2½ cups filling*

*Note:* Chorizo is also delicious formed into patties and fried. The cooked patties make a good breakfast dish.

# Flautas

*Flautas are another form of taco, formed with two overlapping tortillas, filled, rolled, and fried until crisp.*

Soft tortillas
Meat filling (see pages 16-18)
Oil for frying

1. To prepare each flauta, arrange 2 soft tortillas on a flat surface, overlapping one about halfway over the other. Spoon desired amount of meat filling down center length. Roll up, starting with one long side and rolling toward other. Pin closed with wooden picks or small skewers, or hold closed with tongs.
2. Fry in oil in a skillet until crisp. Drain. Eat while hot.

# Enrollados

*Still another type of taco—batter dipped and then deep fried—is named Enrollados. Use one of the fillings on page 17, or try this version, which is a kind of pork picadillo containing potatoes.*

**Filling:**
- ½ pound boneless pork loin (lomo)
- ½ pound potatoes, pared
- 2 tablespoons oil or lard
- 1 cup chopped onion
- 1 cup tomato purée
  Salt and pepper
- 12 soft tortillas
- ¼ cup flour
- 3 eggs, beaten
- ¾ cup oil for frying

**Garnish:**
- ¼ cup shredded Monterey Jack
- 1½ cups canned enchilada sauce
  Avocado slices

1. Prepare filling by cooking pork in a small amount of salted water until tender; shred.
2. Chop potatoes.
3. Heat oil; cook onion in oil until soft (about 5 minutes). Add shredded pork and potatoes. Stir in tomato purée. Season to taste with salt and pepper. Simmer until thick, stirring frequently.
4. Spoon a scoop of this mixture on center of each tortilla. Roll up tortilla; dip in flour and then in beaten eggs.
5. Fry in hot fat until crisp on all sides.
6. Serve hot, sprinkled with shredded cheese, topped with sauce, and garnished with avocado slices.

*12 enrollados*

# Quesadillas

- 1½ cups shredded Monterey Jack or mild Cheddar cheese
- 2 ancho chilies, peeled, seeded, stemmed, and chopped; or 2 or 3 chopped canned jalapeño chilies
- 12 soft corn tortillas
  Oil for frying

1. Combine cheese and chopped chilies.
2. Use as a filling for folded crisp-fried tacos, spooning about 1 heaping tablespoon of filling onto center of each soft tortilla before folding and frying. As taco is fried, cheese will melt and help hold tortilla in folded position.

*12 quesadillas*

# Burritos

*Burritos are a type of taco made with wheat flour tortillas. The filling may be refried beans alone, or combined with meat as in the following recipe.*

- 12 wheat flour tortillas
- 1½ cups hot refried beans (use canned beans or see recipe on page 28)
- 1½ cups hot Ground Beef Filling (see page 16)
  Oil for frying (optional)

1. Spread each tortilla with about 1 tablespoon refried beans, spreading only to about ½ inch of edge. Spoon a heaping tablespoon of ground beef filling along one side. Fold in ends about 1 inch to cover filling, then roll up tortilla starting with side on which meat has been placed. Serve at once.
2. Or, fry in hot oil until crisp, placing each burrito in skillet with open flap on bottom to start, then turning to fry top and sides. Drain on absorbent paper. Serve hot.

*12 burritos*

## TOSTADAS

In the United States we usually think of tostadas as small, crisp wedges of fried tortillas. And so may they also be in Mexico. However, they are just as often full-size tortillas. Whichever size or shape, they are made by frying whole tortillas or wedges in deep hot fat until crisp, then draining well on absorbent paper. They may be eaten hot or cold. The small wedges are often used as "dippers" for guacamole or refritos. Full-size tostadas are used as the base for an open-face taco, to be spread with refritos and liberally piled with an assortment of toppings: cooked meat, shredded cabbage, sliced radishes, chopped onions, shredded cheese, and of course a sauce of tomatoes and/or chilies.

# Totopos

1 small onion, finely chopped
1 tablespoon butter
1 can (15 ounces) kidney beans (undrained)
Salt and pepper
6 tortillas
Oil for frying
Shredded lettuce
2 ripe avocados, peeled, pitted, and sliced
2 cups slivered cooked chicken
3 jalapeño chilies, seeded and thinly sliced, or 3 pickles, thinly sliced
Oil and Vinegar Dressing (see page 66)
1 fresh tomato, sliced
¾ cup shredded Monterey Jack or mild Cheddar cheese

1. Sauté onion in butter in a skillet. Add kidney beans with liquid and cook until liquid is reduced by half.
2. Remove beans from skillet to a bowl. Mash beans and season to taste with salt and pepper.
3. Fry tortillas, one at a time, in oil in a skillet. Drain and cool. Spread tortillas with mashed beans and put on individual plates.
4. Toss lettuce, avocado slices, chicken, and chilies with a small amount of dressing.
5. Pile salad mixture on mashed beans, top with tomato slices, and sprinkle with cheese.

*6 servings*

# Fresh Tomato Sauce

*Following is a recipe for a simple uncooked table sauce which is ideal for topping tacos and tostadas. If preferred, one of the many bottled hot sauces of chilies and/or tomatoes may be used as well.*

2 large ripe tomatoes, peeled and cored
¼ cup chopped onion
2 canned jalapeño chilies, finely chopped (more or less may be used, to taste)
1 tablespoon chopped cilantro (optional)
¼ teaspoon salt
Pepper (optional)

1. Chop tomatoes into small pieces. Add remaining ingredients and allow flavors to blend at least 30 minutes before using.
2. Store in refrigerator.

*About 2 cups sauce*

## ENCHILADAS

Enchiladas are another popular Mexican food based on the tortilla. They are similar to tacos in that the tortillas are wrapped around meat and vegetable fillings. But there is one major difference. The tortillas are first dipped in a sauce and fried quickly in hot oil until the sauce is slightly "set" onto the tortilla before being filled and placed in a casserole. Usually more sauce is then poured over the top and the whole casserole is baked. The final result is a dish in which the tortillas take on an almost pastalike consistency.

Enchiladas may be filled ahead of mealtime and heated just before serving. Preparation of enchiladas is often a somewhat messy procedure, but can be made simpler if carried out in an organized fashion as described below.

*How to dip and fry tortillas for enchiladas:* Before starting to prepare enchiladas, assemble a series of dishes: first, a flat bowl or pan of sauce; next, a small skillet containing hot oil over medium heat on the range; next, a plate or flat bowl in which to place fried tortillas for filling; and finally, the casserole in which the filled enchiladas are to be placed. Have ready a pair of tongs, or a fork, with which to lift tortillas into and out of sauce and oil. Place one tortilla at a time in the sauce, turn to coat both sides, lift with tongs, and shake off excess sauce. Next place sauced tortilla in hot oil and fry about 30 seconds; turn and fry on other side for 30 seconds. Lift with tongs and shake off excess oil, then lay on plate or in flat bowl. It is a good idea to fry at least enough tortillas for one layer in casserole before filling, since the final rolling of the filled tortilla is best achieved with the fingers, so can be quite messy.

## *Swiss Enchiladas*

2 cans (6 ounces each) tomato
    paste
¼ cup coarsely chopped onion
1 clove garlic
1 teaspoon salt
⅛ teaspoon pepper
2 cups water
1 chicken bouillon cube
    Oil for frying
12 soft corn tortillas
1½ cups finely diced cooked chicken
1½ cups shredded cheese (Monterey
    Jack, Chihuahua, or process
    Swiss)
½ cup whipping cream

1. Combine tomato paste, onion, garlic, salt, pepper, and 1 cup of the water in an electric blender. Blend until liquefied.
2. Pour into a medium-size skillet; stir in remaining water and bouillon cube. Bring to boiling and simmer until bouillon cube is dissolved, stirring frequently. Continue to simmer over low heat until smooth and slightly thickened. Remove from heat.
3. Pour about ¼ inch oil into a small skillet and heat to sizzling.
4. To prepare enchiladas, first dip each tortilla into hot sauce, turning to coat both sides; then fry coated tortilla in hot oil, about 30 seconds per side. Remove from oil; drain slightly.
5. Put about 2 tablespoons chicken at one side of tortilla and roll up. Place in a shallow casserole with open flap on bottom. Repeat until all tortillas are filled. Sprinkle with shredded cheese and drizzle with cream. Pour remaining sauce over all.
6. Bake at 350°F about 30 minutes, or until bubbling hot.

*About 6 servings*

# Ranch-Style Enchiladas

**Sauce:**

    5 ancho chilies
    1 clove garlic
    ⅛ teaspoon salt
    1 cup chicken stock or bouillon or
       1¼ cups canned enchilada
       sauce

**Enchiladas:**

    Oil for frying
    12 corn tortillas (6- or 7-inch size)
    2 cups diced cooked chicken or
       pork
    ½ cup chopped onion
       Shredded lettuce

1. To make sauce, toast and peel chilies as directed on page 30; remove stems and seeds. Put into an electric blender with garlic, salt, and chicken broth. Blend until liquefied. Pour into a medium-size skillet and cook about 5 minutes.

2. Pour about ¼ inch oil into a small skillet and heat to sizzling.

3. To prepare enchiladas, first dip each tortilla in hot sauce, turning to coat both sides; they fry coated tortilla in hot oil, about 30 seconds per side. Remove from oil; drain slightly.

4. Put about 2 tablespoons chicken or pork along one side; sprinkle with onion. Roll up and place in a shallow casserole with open flap on bottom. Repeat until all tortillas are filled.

5. When ready to serve, heat in a 350°F oven about 20 minutes.

6. Serve topped with shredded lettuce.

*About 6 servings*

# Cheese Enchiladas with Chili Sauce

    6 dried ancho chilies
    ¼ cup water
    ¼ teaspoon garlic salt
       Oil for frying
    24 soft corn tortillas
    1½ pounds shredded Monterey Jack
    ½ cup chopped onion
    1 teaspoon oregano
    1 cup whipping cream

1. Put chilies into a saucepan with small amount of water; cook until softened. Drain; remove seeds and pith.

2. Put into an electric blender with ¼ cup water. Blend until puréed. Pour into saucepan, add garlic salt, and heat to bubbling.

3. In another saucepan, pour in oil to about ½-inch depth; heat to boiling.

4. Pass tortillas through oil, one at a time, then through warm sauce. Spoon cheese on tortilla and sprinkle with onion and oregano. Roll up and arrange filled tortillas in a single layer in the bottom of a baking dish. Pour a third of the cream over all and sprinkle with a little cheese. Repeat for two more layers.

5. Bake at 350°F about 15 minutes, or until heated through and cheese is melted.

*8 to 10 servings*

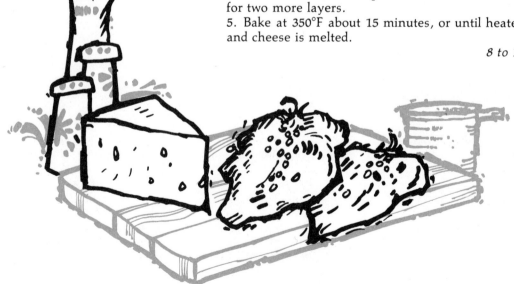

# Chicken Enchiladas

3 cups shredded cooked chicken
    white meat
  Green Chili Sauce (double
    recipe, page 31)
12 tortillas
  Dairy sour cream

1. Lightly toss chicken with ¾ cup sauce.
2. Dip each tortilla in hot sauce, spoon ¼ cup of chicken down center, and roll up. Place enchiladas, open edge down, in a baking dish, then spoon hot sauce over them; cover dish.
3. Set in a 400°F oven about 10 minutes, or until thoroughly heated.
4. Serve with sour cream.

*6 servings*

The following two recipes are for casserole dishes in which tortillas provide the "pasta." During baking they take on a meatlike consistency as they soak up the sauce.

# Pastel de Tortilla

2 large ancho chilies
2 cups canned salsa verde
    mexicana (Mexican green
    tomato sauce)
1 cup chicken stock or bouillon
20 tortillas
  Oil for frying
1 pound diced cooked pork
1 cup cream
1 cup shredded Monterey Jack or
    mild Cheddar cheese

1. Toast and peel chilies as directed on page 30; remove stems and seeds and cut into thin strips.
2. Combine chilies with salsa verde and chicken stock.
3. Meanwhile, slice tortillas into strips and fry in hot oil until crisp; drain on absorbent paper.
4. Layer ingredients in a 2-quart casserole as follows: first ⅓ of fried tortilla strips, next ⅓ of diced pork, then ⅓ of salsa verde mixture. Repeat twice more. Pour cream over all. Sprinkle cheese over top.
5. Heat in a 350°F oven about 30 minutes, or until heated through.

*8 servings*

# Chicken Chalupa

12 corn tortillas
1¼ cups chicken stock or bouillon
1 cup dairy sour cream
¼ cup chopped onion
1 clove garlic, minced
1 to 3 canned jalapeño chilies,
    finely chopped
1 teaspoon salt
2 cups diced cooked chicken
2 cups shredded Monterey Jack or
    mild Cheddar cheese
  Paprika

1. Soak tortillas in 1 cup of the chicken stock.
2. Combine remaining ¼ cup chicken stock, sour cream, onion, garlic, chilies, and salt and stir until well mixed.
3. Layer ingredients in a casserole as follows: single layer of soaked tortillas, chicken, sauce, and then cheese; repeat until all ingredients are used, ending with cheese on top. Sprinkle with paprika.
4. Let stand overnight (or about 8 hours) in refrigerator before baking.
5. Bake at 350°F 1 hour.

*6 to 8 servings*

# TAMALES

Tamales, another popular Mexican specialty food, also combine a corn masa "wrapper" with a spicy meat filling; often they are served with a sauce, as well. But in spite of containing much the same ingredients as tacos and enchiladas, the method of preparation is so different from either of those two Mexican specialties that there seems to be no similarity at all—another example of the ingenuity of Aztec cooking.

For tamales, the corn masa dough is made rich with lard which is beaten until very fluffy before the masa flour is added. This helps produce a light texture in the cooked dough, as contrasted with the very compact texture of tortillas. (Mexican cooks beat the lard with their hands, rather than using a spoon or electric mixer; the heat of the hand helps soften the lard as it is beaten.) The dough is spread onto soft, dry corn husks, filled with meat or poultry, rolled up, and finally steamed until thoroughly cooked. The result is "pockets" of moist dumplinglike dough with a spicy filling.

Homemade tamales are somewhat different than those generally available ready-made. The dough is usually lighter and more moist, with a more distinct corn flavor. A definite advantage of the homemade variety is being able to choose your favorite filling. Ground beef or pork, picadillo, and chicken or turkey with mole sauce are some of the more popular fillings. (See recipes for taco fillings on pages 16–18.) Leftover fillings may be used up, too, to give you a variety of tamales with one recipe of dough.

Two requirements for tamale-making are not universally available throughout the United States: dehydrated masa flour (often called masa harina), for which there is no substitute; and dried corn husks, for which foil or parchment paper squares can be substituted. So, if you can purchase the dehydrated masa flour in a Mexican grocery, by all means try your hand at making some homemade tamales. If possible, use corn-husk wrappers, rather than foil or parchment, for the porous husks permit a more moist cooked dough, and also add flavor to the tamales. In Mexico, and in Mexican specialty stores in the United States, dried corn husks are sold neatly plastic wrapped, ready to use. But you can also save and dry your own, if such a store source is not available.

Dessert tamales, filled with fruits, nuts, or preserves, are popular, too. The dough recipe is much the same as that for meat tamales, with water substituted for the meat stock and a little sugar added to the dough.

Tamale Pie is another way of achieving tamale flavor without so much time-consuming preparation. Two recipes are included here. One is a Mexican version of tamale pie using corn masa dough as the lining and topping for chicken filling. The other is a very Americanized recipe calling for cornmeal batter as a topping for a spicy pork filling.

*To serve tamales:* Tamales may be served with the corn husk wrappers intact, for each diner to remove as he eats. Or, you may remove them ahead of serving time and keep the tamales warm in a casserole. When unwrapped, tamales are delicate, so handle with care.

# Meat or Poultry Tamales

3½ dozen large dry corn husks
1 cup lard
4 cups dehydrated masa flour
    (masa harina)
2½ to 3 cups warm meat or poultry
    stock (or water)
2 teaspoons salt
3½ cups meat or poultry filling of
    your choice (Picadillo, page
    17; Ground Beef Filling, page
    16; or Chicken or Turkey
    Mole Poblano, page 45)

1. Wash corn husks in warm water, put into a saucepan, and cover with boiling water. Let soak at least 30 minutes before using.
2. Beat lard until light and fluffy, using spoon or electric mixer. Gradually beat in masa flour and stock until dough sticks together and has a pastelike consistency. Taste dough before adding salt; if stock is salty you will not need all 2 teaspoons of salt.
3. Shake excess water from each softened corn husk and pat dry on paper towels. Spread about 2 tablespoons tamale dough on center portion of husk, leaving at least a 2-inch margin at both ends and about ½-inch margin at right side. Spoon about 1½ tablespoons filling onto dough. Wrap tamale, overlapping left side first, then right side slightly over left. Fold bottom up and top down.
4. Lay tamales in top section of steamer with open flaps on bottom. (If husks are too short to stay closed, they may be tied with string or thin strips of corn husk.) Tamales may completely fill top section of steamer but should be placed so there are spaces between them for circulation of steam.
5. Steam over simmering water about 1 hour, or until corn husk can be peeled from dough easily.

*3½ dozen tamales*

# Chicken Tamale Pie

*Filling:*
    ¼ cup lard or cooking oil
    1 cup chopped onion
    1 clove garlic, minced
    2 cups (16-ounce can) cooked
        tomatoes
1½ teaspoons salt
    1 tablespoon chili powder
    ½ teaspoon cumin (comino)
    3 cups diced cooked chicken
*Tamale Dough:*
    ½ cup lard
    3 cups dehydrated masa flour
        (masa harina)
    1 teaspoon baking powder
    ½ teaspoon salt
    1 cup chicken stock (or 1 cup
        water plus 1 chicken bouillon
        cube)

1. For filling, heat lard in a large skillet. Add onion and garlic and cook until onion is soft, about 5 minutes. Add tomatoes and seasonings and bring to boiling, stirring until evenly mixed. Reduce heat and simmer about 10 minutes. Stir in chicken and simmer about 5 minutes.
2. For the tamale dough, beat lard until light and fluffy, using spoon or electric mixer. Combine masa flour, baking powder, and salt. Gradually beat flour mixture and chicken stock into lard until dough sticks together and has a pastelike consistency.
3. Grease a 2-quart casserole. Press tamale dough onto bottom and sides of casserole in a layer about ½ inch thick, reserving enough dough to cover top. Pour in prepared filling. Cover filling with remaining dough patted into a layer of same thickness as lining.
4. Bake at 350°F about 1 hour.

*6 to 8 servings*

# Pork Tamale Pie

**Filling:**
- 1½ pounds ground lean pork
- ½ cup chopped onion
- 2 cups cooked tomatoes (19-ounce can)
- 1 clove garlic
- 1 tablespoon chili powder
- 1½ teaspoons salt
- ½ teaspoon oregano
- ¼ teaspoon pepper

**Cornmeal Topping:**
- 1 cup yellow or white cornmeal
- 2 tablespoons flour
- 1 tablespoon sugar
- 2 teaspoons baking powder
- ½ teaspoon salt
- 1 egg
- ½ cup milk
- 1 tablespoon melted shortening, bacon drippings, or oil

1. For the filling, brown pork in a large skillet, crumbling and stirring until all meat is browned.
2. Put onion, some of the tomatoes, garlic, and chili powder into an electric blender; blend to a thick purée. Gradually add remaining tomatoes and continue blending until puréed.
3. Pour tomato purée into skillet with meat. Bring to boiling; reduce heat to simmering. Stir in salt, oregano, and pepper. Cover and simmer 30 minutes.
4. Meanwhile, for cornmeal topping, mix cornmeal with flour, sugar, baking powder, and salt in a bowl.
5. Beat egg slightly; beat in milk and shortening. Add liquid ingredients to dry ingredients all at once and stir lightly, just until all dry ingredients are moistened. Do not beat.
6. Spoon batter over simmering filling.
7. Bake at 425°F 20 to 25 minutes, or until topping is golden brown.

*About 6 servings*

# Dessert Tamales

- 3½ dozen large dry corn husks
- 1 cup lard (or ½ cup lard and ½ cup butter or margarine)
- 4 cups dehydrated masa flour (masa harina)
- 1 cup sugar
- 1 teaspoon salt
- 2½ to 3 cups warm water or fruit
  Date-Pecan Filling (or other fruit or nut filling of your choice)

1. Wash corn husks in warm water, put into a saucepan, and cover with boiling water. Let soak at least 30 minutes before using.
2. Beat lard until light and fluffy, using spoon or electric mixer.
3. Combine masa flour, sugar, and salt. Gradually beat in this mixture and water until dough sticks together and has a pastelike consistency.
4. Shake excess water from each softened corn husk and pat dry on paper towels. Spread about 2 tablespoons tamale dough on center portion of husk, leaving at least a 2-inch margin at both ends and about ½-inch margin at right side. Spoon about 1½ tablespoons filling onto dough. Wrap tamale, overlapping left side first, then right side slightly over left. Fold bottom up and top down.
5. Lay tamales in top section of steamer with open flaps on bottom. (If husks are too short to stay closed, they may be tied with string or thin strips of corn husk.) Tamales may completely fill top section of steamer but should be placed so there are spaces between them for circulation of steam.
6. Steam over simmering water about 1 hour, or until corn husks can be peeled from dough easily.

*3½ dozen tamales*

Date-Pecan Filling: Blend **1 cup brown sugar,** ¼ cup **butter or margarine,** and ½ teaspoon cinnamon until smooth. Add **1 cup chopped pitted dates** and **1 cup chopped pecans;** toss until evenly mixed.

# BEANS AND CHILIES

### BEANS

Beans (frijoles) appear at most Mexican meals, and are often served alongside breakfast eggs, as well. They are also used as fillings for tacos, tamales, and tostadas. To prepare beans "from scratch" is a very simple, if somewhat lengthy process. Following is a basic recipe which produces delicious results. And if you really enjoy your beans, it is well worth the time involved in preparation. On the other hand, very good Mexican-style beans are also available canned, and can be used in the recipes which follow. Or, you may even start with canned cooked kidney beans and continue from that point.

## *Basic Mexican Beans*

**1 pound dried pinto, pink, black, or red kidney beans**
**1 cup chopped onion**
**Water**
**Salt to taste**

1. Wash beans well and put into a large saucepan. Add onion, then add enough water to cover beans completely. Cover, bring water to boiling, reduce heat, and simmer until beans are tender, about 3 hours. Add more water if needed, but add it gradually so water continues to boil.
2. When beans are tender, add salt to taste.
3. Use in recipes calling for cooked beans.

*About 5 to 6 cups cooked beans*

Soupy Beans: Beans prepared as above are sometimes served in soup bowls without further preparation, or with a sprinkling of grated cheese and chopped green onion.

# Refried Beans *(Frijoles Refritos)*

2 to 3 cups cooked beans (see Basic Mexican Beans, page 27; or use canned kidney beans)
½ cup lard or bacon drippings
1 cup chopped onion
1 clove garlic, minced
½ cup cooked tomatoes or tomato sauce
1 teaspoon chili powder
Salt and pepper

1. Mash beans with a potato masher with half of the lard or bacon drippings (drippings make the best-flavored beans).
2. Heat remaining lard or drippings in skillet. Add onion and garlic and cook until onion is soft, about 5 minutes. Add mashed beans and continue cooking until all fat is absorbed by beans, stirring constantly to prevent sticking. Stir in tomatoes, chili powder, and salt and pepper to taste.

*3 to 4 cups beans*

# Hot Bean Dip

¼ cup lard or bacon drippings
1 to 3 canned jalapeño chilies, chopped
1 cup refried beans (see above; or use canned)
½ cup tomato sauce

1. Heat lard in a small skillet or saucepan. Add chopped chilies and fry in hot fat about 5 minutes. Add beans and tomato sauce and stir until well blended.
2. Transfer dip to a small chafing-dish-type server and keep hot during serving. Serve with **tostada chip "dippers."**

*About 1½ cups dip*

## CHILIES

Chilies are an essential ingredient in Mexican cooking, appearing in everything from soup to nuts, quite literally. Recipes for appetizers, soups, casseroles, salads, meats, fish, poultry, eggs, and cocktail nuts call for the addition of chili, so it is impossible to achieve authentic Mexican flavor without them. Because there are so many different varieties of chilies in common use, some basic knowledge of the various types is helpful to the novice Mexican cook.

The fact that chilies are sometimes called peppers is a misnomer. For the podlike chilies, native to the western hemisphere, are not related botanically or in physical appearance to the plant which produces peppercorns, from which our common spice, black pepper, is prepared. Their only similarity is that both offer some degree of "bite" when eaten.

Apparently the Indians who inhabited Mexico before the Spanish conquest, and who originally started cultivating chilies, used them partially for their short-term preservative value. In a cuisine which was rather lacking in animal protein sources, they also lent variety to the cooking. For the different types have quite distinctive flavors, in addition to offering varying degrees of hotness.

These flavor characteristics must be learned through experience, much as wine experts learn to differentiate among the various wines made from similar grapes.

There are more than fifty different varieties of chilies, varying in size from that of a large pea to one almost a foot long. As a general rule, the smaller the chili, the hotter or more "picante" it is. The larger chilies tend to be sweet, and their individual flavors can be distinguished because they don't have so much bite. Even so, when using fresh or dried chilies, it's a good idea to

taste a bit to test the hotness before taking a chance on ruining your food for all but the most iron-coated palate.

Visitors to an open food market in Mexico are greeted by a colorful and aromatic, if somewhat confusing, display of chilies, both fresh and dried. Supermarkets may offer two or three types fresh, another three or four dried, and a whole aisle of chilies in cans, some water-packed and others pickled. These can be put in three general classes. First, there are the chilies used primarily for their bite, most commonly the very hot serrano and the slightly less hot jalapeño. Next are the mild, rather sweet chilies which add lots of flavor to dishes, but not much bite; the most commonly used of this type are the ancho, in both fresh and dried form, the mulatto, and the pasilla. Finally there are what might be called special-use chilies—those which have such distinctive flavor and/or color that dishes have been built around them. The pasilla might also be included here, along with the chipotle and morita, which are most often used in the pickled form.

## CHILIES IN THE UNITED STATES

In the United States several fresh chilies are available in season in western and southwestern states, as well as in Mexican neighborhoods or specialty stores in large cities. Dried chilies, packaged in plastic or cellophane, are available the year around in these locations. But as a general rule in the rest of the United States only two types can be found, and both of these are canned.

Most familiar are the bottled "hot peppers" which are usually the small, quite hot jalapeño chilies in pickle brine. These chilies are deep green, conical in shape, and about one to two inches long. Also sometimes bottled as hot peppers are the cascabel chilies: small, pale green, rather round or heart-shaped pods about one to one and one-half inches wide and long. Since both types are usually packed in glass jars, they are easy for the uninitiated chili buyer to recognize. Both may be used in recipes in this book calling for jalapeño chilies.

The other type of chili sold in many supermarkets throughout the United States is labeled "peeled green chilies" or "peeled California green chilies." These have a much larger pod, up to six or seven inches long and about one and one-half to two inches wide at the top, tapering to a point at the bottom. They are usually mild and sweet, and only slightly hot. This is the type appropriate for stuffing as Chilies Rellenos. They can also be substituted for ancho chilies in recipes calling for that type, for they are about equal in hotness, even though the flavors differ.

If none of these types is available in your area, in all recipes calling for chilies, you may substitute either Tabasco or chili powder. Tabasco is made from the very hottest chilies, so that two or three drops will be sufficient substitution for one jalapeño chili.

Chili powders in the United States are a blend of two or more hot to medium-hot chilies, plus other spices like oregano and cumin. Thus chili powders tend to vary. And it may be that you will have to do a little experimenting and a lot of tasting to decide just how much to use for your taste. When using chili powder, it is well to remember that the whole flavor doesn't develop immediately, so it is best to add less than you may think is needed, simmer your sauce a while, taste, then add more if needed.

For Chilies Rellenos, if peeled green chilies are not available, green bell peppers may be substituted. Even though the flavors are different, a delicious dish will result.

Following in this section are recipes which depend upon chilies as the major ingredient rather than simply a flavoring. The two sauces are basic, typical of those served as regular daily table condiments with Mexican meals. Chilies Rellenos, of course, are stuffed chilies, a dish with wide renown. Chili con Queso is probably best known in the United States as a dip, though in Mexico it might be served as a supper main dish, or a first course. Two types are suggested. The first calls for the traditional cream cheese and green chilies; the second is an Americanized version made with a sharper cheese and hotter chili.

*How to prepare fresh chilies for cooking:* Wash chilies and pat dry. If preparing a large number of big chilies, place on a broiler pan; place pan under broiler flame and roast chilies until well-blistered, turning to roast on all sides. For two or three chilies, or for the smaller varieties, roast in a small skillet over high heat until skins pop; chilies will be almost black. Remove from broiler or skillet and put into a plastic bag. Let stand a few minutes, then peel with sharp knife, beginning at the blossom end and working toward stem. Cut a slit in side of each chili and scoop out seeds and veins. If using for Chilies Rellenos, leave stems on to use as "handles." Otherwise, cut around stem with sharp knife and remove. *Note:* Wash hands with soap and water after handling fresh or dried chilies, as the small amount left on hands can burn if rubbed into eyes, or a small cut.

*How to prepare dried chilies for cooking:* Wash chilies and pat dry. Cut open and remove seeds, veins, and stems. Place in a small amount of water and boil until soft, about 10 minutes. Chop or blend as directed in recipe. Save water in which the chilies were boiled to use in whatever sauce you are preparing. Wash hands (see Note above).

*How to use canned "Hot Peppers":* These chilies may simply be chopped and used as they come from can or jar. To somewhat reduce the hotness, if desired, remove seeds and stems and rinse in cold water before chopping. Wash hands (see Note above).

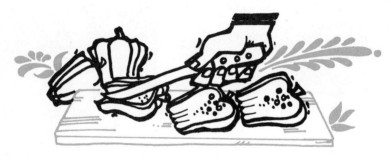

# Chili con Queso

  2 tablespoons butter or margarine
  ½ cup finely chopped onion
  1 cup chopped peeled fresh
      tomatoes
  1 cup chopped peeled fresh green
      California chilies or canned
      peeled green chilies
  1 package (8 ounces) cream cheese
  ¾ cup whipping cream
    Salt and pepper
    Crisp tortilla chips

1. Melt butter in a large skillet. Add onion and cook about 5 minutes, or until soft. Add tomatoes and chilies and cook about 10 minutes, stirring occasionally.
2. Cut cheese into chunks and stir into skillet mixture. When cheese melts, stir in cream. Add salt and pepper to taste.
3. Serve hot over toasted tortilla chips, or keep warm in chafing dish and serve as a dip with tortilla chips.

*About 2½ cups dip*

Variation: Substitute 1 or 2 chopped jalapeño chilies for the California green chilies and 8 ounces shredded sharp Cheddar cheese for the cream cheese.

# Red Chili Sauce

  4 fresh or dried ancho chilies
  1 cup canned tomatoes with juice
  1 cup chopped onion
  1 clove garlic
  1 teaspoon oregano
  ¼ teaspoon cumin (comino)
  ¼ cup olive oil
    Salt and pepper
  1 tablespoon vinegar
    Few drops Tabasco

1. Prepare the chilies (see this page). Put prepared chilies, tomatoes, onion, garlic, oregano, and cumin into an electric blender and blend to a purée.
2. Heat oil in a skillet. Add puréed sauce and cook about 10 minutes. Stir in salt and pepper to taste, then vinegar and Tabasco to taste. Cool before serving.

*About 2 cups sauce*

# Green Chili Sauce

1 cup chopped canned peeled green
    chilies
1 cup canned Mexican green
    tomatoes (tomatillos)
¼ cup chopped fresh parsley
¼ cup chopped onion
1 clove garlic
1 canned jalapeño chili, chopped
    Salt and pepper
¼ cup olive oil

1. Put green chilies, green tomatoes, parsley, onion, garlic, and jalapeño chili into an electric blender. Blend to a purée. Add salt and pepper to taste.
2. Heat oil in skillet. Add puréed sauce and cook about 5 minutes, stirring constantly. Cool before serving.

*About 2 cups sauce*

A number of different fillings can be used to make Chilies Rellenos (stuffed chilies). Most commonly Picadillo or a soft, melty cheese such as Monterey Jack provides the stuffing. Sometimes refried beans are used. If fresh green California chilies are available, by all means use them. Or, these same chilies are usually available canned, in Mexican grocery stores. Otherwise, choose green bell peppers.

# Chilies Rellenos

6 fresh or canned California green
    chilies (see Note) or 6 green
    bell peppers
2 cups Picadillo (see page 17) or ½
    pound Monterey Jack or mild
    Cheddar cheese
2 eggs, separated
    Flour
    Oil for frying
*Sauce:*
1 cup chopped onion
1 clove garlic, minced
2 cups canned tomato sauce
1 tablespoon oil
1 cup chicken stock, or water plus
    1 chicken bouillon cube
    Salt and pepper

1. Make a slit in the side of each chili and with a spoon carefully remove seeds and pith, leaving stems intact. (If using peppers, cut around stem with a sharp knife, leaving attached at one side, if possible; slit side. Remove seeds and pith.)
2. Fill chilies with desired filling.
3. Beat egg whites until stiff, not dry, peaks form; beat egg yolks until thick and lemon colored. Fold whites into yolks. Dust chilies with flour, then dip into beaten egg to coat on all sides.
4. Heat oil (about 1-inch depth) in a heavy skillet or large heavy saucepan to about 350°F. Fry stuffed chilies in hot oil, turning to brown on all sides. Stems may be used as "handles" to help turn the chilies.
5. Drain on absorbent paper and set aside while preparing sauce.
6. For sauce, put onion, garlic, and tomato sauce into an electric blender. Blend until liquefied.
7. Heat 1 tablespoon oil in skillet. Cook sauce in oil about 5 minutes. Stir in chicken stock. Season to taste with salt and pepper.
8. Place fried stuffed chilies in sauce and cook a few minutes until they reach serving temperature.

*6 servings*

*Note:* If chilies are very hot, they may be soaked in a solution of 1 quart water, 1 tablespoon salt, and 1 tablespoon vinegar for an hour before using.

# Stuffed Peppers with Nogada Sauce
## (Chilies Rellenos en Nogada)

6 medium green peppers
3 tablespoons lard
2 cloves garlic, minced
¼ cup chopped onion
1 pound lean ground pork
½ pound ham with fat, ground
2 cups chopped ripe tomatoes
2 tablespoons snipped parsley
3 tablespoons cider vinegar
½ teaspoon vanilla extract
2 tablespoons sugar
4 whole cloves, crushed
5 peppercorns, crushed
¼ teaspoon nutmeg
⅛ teaspoon powdered saffron
¼ cup finely chopped almonds
¼ cup dark seedless raisins
1 teaspoon chopped capers
2 tablespoons chopped candied
   lemon peel
¼ cup pitted chopped green olives
   Nogada Sauce (see below)
   Flour
2 eggs, beaten
   Lard for deep frying, heated to
   365°F (see Note)
   Pomegranate seeds

1. Cut out stems of peppers; remove seeds and membrane. Place peppers in a large saucepan; cover with boiling water, bring to boiling, and cook about 2 minutes. Drain and invert peppers on absorbent paper.
2. Heat 3 tablespoons lard in a heavy skillet; add garlic, onion, and meat. Cook until meat is browned, stirring occasionally.
3. Meanwhile, mix tomatoes, parsley, vinegar, vanilla extract, sugar, and spices.
4. Add tomato mixture to meat along with almonds, raisins, capers, lemon peel, and olives; stir. Cook over low heat, stirring frequently, until mixture is almost dry (30 to 40 minutes).
5. Meanwhile, prepare Nogada Sauce.
6. Spoon filling into peppers, packing lightly so mixture will remain in cavities during frying.
7. Roll peppers in flour, coating entire surface. Dip in beaten eggs.
8. Fry peppers in hot deep fat until coating is golden. Remove peppers with a slotted spoon and drain on absorbent paper.
9. Arrange stuffed peppers on a serving plate and top with Nogada Sauce. Sprinkle with pomegranate seeds.

*6 servings*

*Note:* If desired, use 2 inches of fat in a deep skillet, heat to 365°F, and fry peppers, turning to brown evenly.

# Nogada Sauce

1 cup walnuts, ground
½ clove garlic, ground
5 peppercorns, crushed
¼ cup fine dry bread crumbs
2 tablespoons sugar
½ teaspoon salt
2 tablespoons cider vinegar
6 to 8 tablespoons water

Mix walnuts, garlic, peppercorns, crumbs, sugar, and salt. Add to vinegar, then stir in enough water to make a very thick sauce. Let stand 30 minutes.

**Pork Slices in Mole Verde, 40,** served with tortillas and beer, is a main-dish favorite.

# MAIN DISH FAVORITES

Entrées of meat, poultry, fish, and eggs are just as well-loved in Mexico as in the United States. But there's not the great emphasis placed on meat in the Mexican menu that there is in the U.S. These foods are relatively expensive in Mexico, so are used rather sparingly, with sauces to stretch as well as to season. Then too, the other dishes in the traditional Mexican menu are so interesting and flavorful in their own right that they tend to take some of the starring role from meat.

Middle- and upper-income families eat meat, fish, and poultry dishes daily. But those on the lower end of the economic scale may eat these quite infrequently. And when such foods are included in a recipe, the amount may be very small. A typical taco or tamale, for example, might well contain but a teaspoonful of meat, with the major source of protein, as well as bulk, being beans and the masa dough itself.

Probably because of this lack of emphasis on animal protein as the focus of the meal, the cuts of meat available are quite limited. A Mexican housewife may simply purchase so many kilos of

"carne de res" (beef), or "carne de cerdo" (pork). Her recipe may call just for "carne" (meat) without specifying beef, pork, chicken, turkey, etc. For lower-income families this meat is invariably boiled until tender, shredded, then recooked with chilies (partly for their preservative value, as well as for flavor) then combined with vegetables. The resulting flavorful mixture resembling Picadillo (page 17) will then be used as filling for tortillas and tostadas.

Upper- and middle-income families usually prepare their meats, fish, and poultry in a spicy sauce, which reflects both the Aztec and Spanish ancestry of so much Mexican cooking. Even the eggs have a Mexican accent. Some of the best-loved recipes of this type follow. Pork takes the lead among the meats, probably because it is outstandingly lean and delicious. Chicken and turkey are plentiful, too. And the variety of fish is almost endless, for Mexico has many hundreds of miles of seacoast, and is noted for its excellent deep-sea fishing.

From the eastern coast of Mexico comes **Red Snapper Veracruz Style, 47.**

# Beef Stew (Caldillo)

3 tablespoons lard or vegetable oil
3 pounds lean beef, cut in ½-inch
  cubes
1 large onion, finely chopped
1 clove garlic, minced
3 fresh ripe tomatoes, peeled,
  seeded, and chopped
2 cans (4 ounces each) mild red
  chilies, drained and puréed
2 cups beef broth
2 teaspoons salt
⅛ teaspoon pepper
½ teaspoon oregano

1. Heat lard in a large skillet. Brown meat quickly on all sides. Remove beef from fat and set aside.
2. Add onion and garlic to fat in skillet; cook until onion is soft. Remove from fat and add to beef.
3. Cook tomato in fat in skillet, adding more fat if necessary. Return meat and onion to skillet. Add chili purée, beef broth, and seasonings; stir. Cover; bring to boiling, reduce heat, and cook over low heat about 2 hours, or until meat is tender.

*6 to 8 servings*

# Mexican Beef Stew

2 pounds beef for stew, cut in
  2-inch chunks
1 large onion, chopped
1 clove garlic, minced
1 green pepper, cut in strips
1 cup canned tomato sauce
1 canned chipotle chili, finely
  chopped
1 tablespoon vinegar
1½ teaspoons salt
1 teaspoon oregano
3 cups cubed pared potatoes
4 or 5 carrots, pared and cut in
  strips
  Beef stock, or water plus beef
  bouillon cube
2 tablespoons flour

1. Put meat into a Dutch oven or large kettle. Add onion, garlic, green pepper, tomato sauce, chili, vinegar, salt, and oregano. Cover and bring to boiling; reduce heat and simmer 2½ hours, stirring occasionally.
2. Add potatoes and carrots to meat mixture. If more liquid seems needed, add up to 1 cup beef stock. Cover and cook about 30 minutes, or until meat and vegetables are tender.
3. Sprinkle flour over stew and stir in; continue to cook until sauce is thickened.

*About 8 servings*

# Beefsteak à la Mexicana

2 pounds very thinly sliced tender
  beef (cubed steaks may be
  used)
  Salt, pepper, and garlic salt
  Fat
1 pound fresh tomatoes, peeled,
  cored, and chopped
1 cup chopped onion
4 jalapeño chilies, seeded and
  chopped

1. Sprinkle beef with salt, pepper, and garlic salt on both sides.
2. Pan-fry meat quickly in a small amount of hot fat in a skillet (about 2 minutes per side). Smother with chopped tomatoes, onion, and chilies. Cover skillet and cook over low heat about 15 minutes. Serve at once.

*4 to 6 servings*

# Mexican Meatballs *(Albóndigas)*

*Mexican meatballs often are centered with a chunk of hard-cooked egg as suggested in this recipe. Serve as a meat entrée, or prepare small-size meatballs as a party hors d'oeuvre.*

**Sauce:**
- ½ cup chopped onion
- 1 clove garlic, minced
- ¼ cup oil or lard
- 1 cup tomato sauce
- 2 cups beef broth, or 2 cups water plus 2 beef bouillon cubes
- 1 teaspoon salt
- ½ teaspoon oregano
- ½ teaspoon cumin (comino)
- 2 chipotle chilies, chopped

**Meatballs:**
- 1 pound ground beef
- ½ pound ground pork
- ¼ pound ground cooked ham
- ½ cup chopped onion
- 2 slices dry bread
- ¼ cup milk
- 1 egg
- 1½ teaspoons salt
- ¼ teaspoon pepper
- 2 canned chipotle chilies, chopped
- 2 hard-cooked eggs, coarsely diced (optional)

1. For sauce, cook onion and garlic in hot oil in a large skillet until onion is soft. Add remaining sauce ingredients and heat to boiling, stirring constantly. Reduce heat and let simmer while preparing meatballs.
2. For meatballs, combine beef, pork, ham, and onion.
3. Tear bread into chunks and soak in milk.
4. Beat egg slightly and add salt, pepper, and chopped chilies. Add egg mixture and bread-milk mixture to meat; mix well.
5. Form into balls about 1½ inches in diameter. If desired, press a chunk of hard-cooked egg into center of each meatball.
6. Put meatballs into simmering sauce; cover and simmer 1 hour.

*25 to 30 large meatballs (or about 75 small appetizer-size meatballs)*

# Mexican Meat Loaf

- 1 pound ground beef
- ½ pound ground pork
- ½ cup chopped onion
- ⅔ cup uncooked oats
- 1 egg, beaten
- 1 teaspoon salt
- ¼ teaspoon pepper
- 1 cup Red Chili Sauce (see page 30) or canned enchilada or taco sauce
- 2 hard-cooked eggs, cut in half lengthwise
- ¼ cup sliced pimento-stuffed green olives

1. Combine ground beef, ground pork, onion, oats, beaten egg, salt, pepper, and ½ cup of the sauce, mixing until evenly blended.
2. Pack half of the meat mixture into an 8×4×2-inch loaf pan. Arrange hard-cooked eggs in a row down center of loaf. Arrange olive slices on either side of eggs; press eggs and olives slightly into meat mixture. Cover with remaining half of meat mixture. Pour remaining ½ cup sauce over top.
3. Bake at 350°F 1 hour.

*6 servings*

# Green Chili Meat Loaf

1½ pounds ground beef
1 cup soft bread crumbs
1 cup canned undrained tomatoes
1 can (4 ounces) green chilies, drained, seeded, and chopped
3 tablespoons dried onion flakes
1¼ teaspoons salt
¼ teaspoon garlic salt

1. Combine all ingredients thoroughly. Turn into a 9×5×3-inch loaf dish and press lightly.
2. Bake at 375°F 1 hour.

*About 6 servings*

# Chili con Carne with Beans

1 pound boneless beef, cut in 1-inch cubes
1 pound boneless pork, cut in 1-inch cubes
3 tablespoons lard
1 cup beef broth
1 teaspoon salt
1 to 2 tablespoons chili powder
2 cloves garlic, minced
2 tablespoons lard
1 large onion, coarsely chopped
3 fresh tomatoes, peeled, seeded, and cut in pieces
1 can (16 ounces) white beans, drained
1 can (15 ounces) red kidney beans, drained

1. Brown meat in 3 tablespoons lard in a large skillet. Add broth; cover and cook 30 minutes.
2. Add salt, chili powder, and garlic; mix. Cook covered until meat is tender (about 1 hour).
3. Meanwhile, heat 2 tablespoons lard in a skillet. Add onion and tomato; mix well. Cover and cook until vegetables are soft. Purée vegetables.
4. Add purée and beans to meat; mix well. Heat thoroughly.

*6 to 8 servings*

# Taco Skillet Casserole

1½ pounds ground beef
½ cup chopped onion
1 clove garlic, minced
1 teaspoon salt
¼ teaspoon pepper
1 teaspoon chili powder (see Note)
2 cups canned tomato sauce (see Note)
8 tortillas, cut into ½-inch strips
Oil for frying
½ cup shredded Monterey Jack or mild Cheddar cheese
Shredded lettuce

1. Crumble ground beef into a large skillet and brown well. If beef is very fat, pour off excess fat. Add onion and garlic and cook about 5 minutes, until onion is soft, stirring frequently. Stir in salt, pepper, chili powder, and tomato sauce and continue cooking over low heat about 15 minutes longer.
2. Meanwhile, in a separate skillet, fry tortilla strips in hot oil a few minutes until slightly crisped. Drain on absorbent paper. Stir tortilla strips into meat mixture and cook about 5 minutes longer, stirring frequently to prevent sticking. Sprinkle with cheese. As soon as cheese melts, remove from heat and serve. Top each serving with shredded lettuce.

*6 servings*

Note: **2 cups canned taco** or **enchilada sauce** may be substituted for chili powder and tomato sauce, if preferred.

# Cheese Ball Casserole

1 pound ground lean pork
½ pound smoked ham, ground
1 green pepper, finely chopped
1 small onion, finely chopped
3 cloves garlic, minced
2 tablespoons snipped parsley
1 can (16 ounces) tomatoes, well drained
2 tablespoons tomato juice
2 teaspoons sugar
½ teaspoon salt
¼ teaspoon pepper
½ cup dark seedless raisins
¼ cup chopped green olives
1 tablespoon capers
2 cups shredded tortillas
½ pound sharp Cheddar cheese, thinly sliced
1 egg, beaten
Tortillas

1. Cook pork in a skillet until no longer pink. Mix in remaining ingredients, except cheese, egg, and whole tortillas. Heat for about 20 minutes, stirring occasionally.
2. Meanwhile, cover bottom and sides of a 1½-quart casserole with overlapping cheese slices.
3. When meat mixture is heated, quickly stir in egg and spoon into lined casserole. Around edge of dish overlap small pieces (quarters) of tortillas and remaining cheese slices.
4. Set in a 325°F oven 15 minutes, or until cheese is bubbly.
5. If desired, garnish center with green pepper strips and parsley arranged to form a flower. Serve with warm tortillas.

*8 servings*

# Empanadas

**Picadillo:**
½ pound coarsely chopped beef
½ pound coarsely chopped pork
½ cup chopped onion
1 small clove garlic, minced
½ cup chopped raw apple
¾ cup chopped canned tomatoes
¼ cup raisins
¾ teaspoon salt
⅛ teaspoon pepper
Dash ground cinnamon
Dash ground cloves
¼ cup chopped almonds
**Pastry:**
4 cups all-purpose flour
1¼ teaspoons salt
1⅓ cups lard or shortening
⅔ cup icy cold water (about)

1. For picadillo, cook beef and pork together in large skillet until well browned. Add onion and garlic and cook until onion is soft. Add remaining ingredients, except almonds, and simmer 15 to 20 minutes longer until flavors are well blended.
2. Stir in almonds. Cool.
3. For pastry, mix flour and salt in a bowl. Cut in lard until mixture resembles coarse crumbs. Sprinkle water over flour mixture, stirring lightly with a fork until all dry ingredients hold together. Divide dough in four portions.
4. On a lightly floured surface, roll one portion of dough at a time to ⅛-inch thickness.
5. Using a 5-inch cardboard circle as a pattern, cut rounds of pastry with a knife. Place a rounded spoonful of filling in center of each round. Fold one side over filling to meet opposite side. Seal by dampening inside edges of pastry and pressing together with tines of fork.
6. Place empanadas on a baking sheet. Bake at 400°F 15 to 20 minutes, or until lightly browned. Or fry in **fat for deep frying** heated to 365°F until browned (about 3 minutes); turn once.

*24 to 30 empanadas*

# Lamb Mayan Style

*The sauce for this dish contains two ingredients typical of Mayan dishes from Yucatan: pepitas (pumpkin seeds), generally available in the United States in the roasted, salted form prepared as a cocktail snack, and annatto seeds (also called achiote). The latter would be available in Mexican specialty sections of large supermarkets and in Mexican grocery stores.*

2 pounds boneless lamb for stew, cut in 2-inch chunks
½ cup chopped onion
1 clove garlic, minced
1 cup canned tomatoes, chopped
1 teaspoon salt
¼ teaspoon pepper
　　Water
1 cup pepitas
1 tablespoon annatto seeds
2 tablespoons oil
1 tablespoon lemon juice

1. Put lamb, onion, garlic, tomatoes, salt, and pepper into a Dutch oven or heavy saucepot; mix well. Add water to cover. Bring to boiling, reduce heat, cover, and simmer until meat is tender (about 2 hours).
2. Meanwhile, combine pepitas and annatto seeds in an electric blender and blend until pulverized.
3. Fry mixture in a small amount of hot oil in a small skillet 2 or 3 minutes, stirring constantly. Stir into the sauce with meat. Stir in lemon juice. Serve with **cooked rice.**

*6 servings*

The "porkers" in Mexico are long and lanky compared to their North American cousins. As a result, they produce pork loin comparable in tenderness and juiciness to our roast beef. It is sold boneless as the whole loin, called simply "lomo." Lomo is usually cooked in a sauce, sometimes whole, but just as often cut into large chunks and combined with vegetables or fruit. Three lomo recipes follow.

# Lomo of Pork with Pineapple

1 tablespoon lard or oil
3 pounds pork loin, boneless, cut in 2-inch chunks
1 cup chopped onion
2 cups pineapple chunks (a 15¼-ounce can) with juice
1 cup beef stock, or 1 cup water plus 1 beef bouillon cube
¼ cup dry sherry
⅓ cup sliced pimento
1 fresh tomato, peeled and chopped
½ teaspoon chili powder
　　Salt and pepper
2 tablespoons flour

1. Heat lard in a large, heavy skillet. Add meat and brown well on all sides. Add onion and cook about 5 minutes, or until soft.
2. Add pineapple with juice, beef stock, sherry, pimento, tomato, and chili powder to the skillet; stir until well mixed. Bring to boiling, reduce heat to simmering, and add salt and pepper to taste. Cover and simmer until meat is tender, about 1½ hours; stir occasionally to prevent sticking.
3. Just before serving, sprinkle flour over simmering sauce and stir in; cook and stir until sauce is thickened. Serve over **hot rice.**

*6 to 8 servings*

# Lomo of Pork in Red Adobo

3 pounds pork loin, boneless
1 onion, stuck with 1 clove
1 bay leaf
1 teaspoon salt
Water
*Adobo Sauce:*
6 fresh or dried ancho chilies
1 cup coarsely chopped onion
1 clove garlic
1 cup canned tomatoes
½ teaspoon oregano
½ teaspoon cumin (comino)
2 tablespoons lard or oil
1½ cups pork stock
Salt and pepper
1 avocado (optional)

1. Put pork, onion stuck with clove, bay leaf, and salt into large kettle or Dutch oven; cover with water. Cover kettle and cook until pork is tender, about 1½ hours.
2. Remove pork from stock; strain stock and save, discarding onion and bay leaf. Slice pork into 1-inch slices and return to kettle.
3. For adobo sauce, first prepare chilies (see page 30). Put prepared chilies, onion, garlic, tomatoes, oregano, and cumin into an electric blender. Blend to a thick purée.
4. Heat lard in skillet. Add purée and cook about 5 minutes, stirring constantly. Stir in pork stock. Season to taste with salt and pepper.
5. Pour sauce over sliced pork in kettle. Cook, uncovered, over low heat for about 30 minutes, or until sauce thickens and coats the meat.
6. Peel and slice avocado. Arrange sliced meat on platter. Garnish with avocado slices, if desired.

*6 to 8 servings*

# Whole Lomo of Pork in Tomato Sauce

1 pork loin roast, boneless (3 to 4 pounds)
1 can (6 ounces) tomato paste
¼ cup chopped onion
1 canned chipotle chili, very finely chopped; or 2 teaspoons chili powder
1 clove garlic, minced
1 teaspoon salt
¼ teaspoon pepper
1½ cups chicken stock, or 1½ cups hot water plus 2 chicken bouillon cubes
1 cup dairy sour cream

1. Put pork loin into a shallow baking pan; if necessary, cut in half so meat will fit into pan.
2. Combine tomato paste, onion, chili, garlic, salt, and pepper in a saucepan. Stir in chicken stock. Cook about 5 minutes.
3. Pour liquid over meat in pan.
4. Bake at 325°F about 1¼ hours. Occasionally spoon sauce over meat during baking, and check to see if additional water is needed to prevent drying.
5. When meat is tender, remove to serving platter.
6. Stir sour cream into sauce remaining in pan; warm slightly but do not boil. Pour over meat on platter.
7. To serve, slice meat about ¾ inch thick.

*10 to 12 servings*

# Pork and Green Tomato Stew

2½ pounds lean pork, cut in 1-inch
  cubes
1 tablespoon vegetable oil
1 onion, chopped
2 cloves garlic, minced
1 can (12 ounces) Mexican green
  tomatoes (tomatillos), drained
  and chopped
2 cans (4 ounces each) green
  chilies, drained, seeded, and
  chopped
1 tablespoon dried cilantro leaves
1 teaspoon marjoram
1 teaspoon salt
½ cup water
  Cooked rice
  Dairy sour cream

1. Brown meat in oil in a large skillet. Push meat to sides of skillet; add onion and garlic and cook until onion is soft. Add green tomatoes, chilies, cilantro, marjoram, salt, and water; mix well. Cover; bring to boiling, reduce heat, and cook until meat is tender (about 2 hours).
2. Serve with rice and top with dollops of sour cream.

*6 to 8 servings*

# Chili with Pork

2 pounds lean pork, cut in 1-inch
  cubes
2 tablespoons flour
1 tablespoon chili powder
1½ teaspoons salt
½ teaspoon pepper
1 teaspoon sugar
½ teaspoon cumin (comino) seed
1 clove garlic, minced
2 cans (10 ounces each) mild
  enchilada sauce
2 cups water

1. Brown pork in a heavy skillet. Stir in flour and chili powder. Add remaining seasonings, sauce, and water. Bring to boiling; cover and simmer about 2 hours.
2. Serve with cooked rice and Mexican Beans (page 27), if desired.

*About 8 servings*

# Pork Slices in Mole Verde

½ cup finely chopped onion
¼ cup finely chopped blanched
  almonds
2 tablespoons vegetable oil
2 cans (10 ounces each) Mexican
  green tomatoes (tomatillos)
1 tablespoon minced fresh
  coriander (cilantro) or 1
  teaspoon dried coriander
1 to 3 tablespoons minced canned
  green chilies

1. Combine onion, almonds, and oil in a saucepan. Cook over medium heat until onion is soft.
2. Turn contents of cans of green tomatoes into an electric blender and blend until smooth (or force green tomatoes through a sieve).
3. Add purée to onion mixture and stir in coriander, chilies (to taste), and stock. Bring to boiling, reduce heat, and simmer, uncovered, until reduced to 2½ cups; stir occasionally.
4. Arrange meat in a large skillet, sprinkle with salt to taste, and pour sauce over meat. Cover, bring slowly to boiling,

2 cups chicken stock, or 2 cups
    water, plus 2 chicken bouillon
    cubes
6 to 8 slices cooked pork loin roast
    Salt
    Small lettuce leaves
    Whole pickled mild chilies
    Dairy sour cream

reduce heat, and simmer about 10 minutes, or until thoroughly heated.

5. Arrange sauced meat on a platter. Garnish with lettuce and chilies. Accompany with sour cream.

*6 to 8 servings*

# Dried Lima Casserole

*More Mexican-style beans—limas, this time. This dish makes a delectable luncheon or supper main dish, quite out of the ordinary.*

1 pound dried lima beans
1 large onion, sliced
¼ cup lard or oil
¼ pound chorizo or Italian-style
    sausage meat
¼ pound diced ham
1 cup canned enchilada sauce
½ cup shredded Monterey Jack

1. Soak lima beans in water to cover for 1 hour. Bring to boiling, reduce heat, and cook until tender; add more water if necessary.

2. Meanwhile, cook onion in lard until soft (about 5 minutes). If using sausage in casing, remove from casing and add to onion, crumbling slightly. Cook and stir until well browned. Add ham and enchilada sauce; cover and cook about 30 minutes.

3. Skim off excess fat. Add cooked beans and continue cooking about 15 minutes longer to blend flavors. Sprinkle with cheese just before serving.

*6 to 8 servings*

*Note:* This skillet-type casserole dish can be transferred to a baking dish before the cheese is sprinkled on top. It may then be refrigerated for later serving. Heat in a 350°F oven 20 to 30 minutes, or until bubbling.

# Pork and Beans Mexican Style

*This Mexican-style pork-and-beans dish offers more pork than the North American variety. Therefore it's definitely an entrée.*

¼ pound sliced bacon
¼ pound boneless pork loin
    (lomo) or pork tenderloin,
    cubed
¼ pound ham, cubed
1 large onion, sliced
1½ cups fresh or canned, peeled,
    diced tomatoes
1 teaspoon chili powder
½ teaspoon cumin (comino)
½ teaspoon oregano
2 cups cooked pinto or kidney
    beans (canned or prepared as
    directed on page 27)
12 ounces beer

1. Cook bacon until crisp; drain and crumble. In bacon fat brown pork and ham. Add onion; cover and cook until soft (about 5 minutes).

2. Add tomatoes, chili powder, cumin, oregano, and the crumbled bacon. Add cooked beans; bring to boiling. Gradually stir in beer. Continue to simmer over low heat about 1 hour, or until pork is well done and mixture is consistency of rich stew, stirring occasionally.

3. Serve in bowls as a stew, or with hot, soft tortillas to make tacos.

*4 to 6 servings*

# Tongue in Almond Sauce

2 veal tongues (about 2½ pounds each)
1 medium onion, stuck with 2 or 3 cloves
1 stalk celery with leaves
1 bay leaf
6 peppercorns
2 teaspoons salt
Water

Almond Sauce:
2 fresh or dried ancho chilies
½ cup canned tomatoes with juice
½ cup whole blanched almonds
½ cup raisins
1 slice bread, torn in pieces
2 tablespoons lard or oil
2 cups tongue stock
Salt and pepper
¼ cup blanched slivered almonds

1. Put tongues, onion stuck with cloves, celery, bay leaf, peppercorns, and salt into a Dutch oven or kettle. Cover with water. Cover Dutch oven, bring to boiling, and cook until meat is tender, about 2 hours. Allow to cool in liquid.
2. Remove skin from cooled tongues, trim off roots, and slice meat into ½-inch slices. Strain stock in which meat was cooked and save, discarding onion, celery, and bay leaf. Return sliced meat to kettle.
3. For almond sauce, first prepare chilies (see page 30). Put chilies, tomatoes, the whole almonds, ¼ cup of the raisins, and the bread into an electric blender. Blend to a thick purée.
4. Heat lard in a skillet. Add the puréed mixture and cook about 5 minutes. Stir in tongue stock and remaining ¼ cup raisins. Cook about 5 minutes, stirring constantly. Season to taste with salt and pepper.
5. Pour sauce over sliced meat in Dutch oven and simmer until meat is heated through.
6. Transfer meat and sauce to platter and garnish with slivered almonds.

*8 to 10 servings*

# Chicken Tablecloth Stainer

*Mexicans love to give humorous names to foods, and this particular dish is undoubtedly well-named. The reason becomes obvious when you see the deep red color of the sauce, caused by the dark pasilla chilies called for in the recipe. This same sauce is often used with pork, and occasionally both pork and chicken are combined in the same recipe.*

2 frying chickens (about 2½ pounds each), cut in serving pieces
½ pound link sausages
½ cup canned pineapple chunks, drained
1 apple, pared, cored, and sliced
1 large, firm banana, sliced

Sauce:
2 fresh or dried ancho chilies and 2 fresh or dried pasilla chilies, or 1 tablespoon chili powder
1 cup coarsely chopped onion
1 clove garlic
2 cups (16-ounce can) tomatoes with juice
½ cup whole blanched almonds
¼ teaspoon cinnamon
⅛ teaspoon cloves
2 cups chicken stock, or 2 cups water plus 2 chicken bouillon cubes
Salt and pepper

1. Put chicken pieces into a Dutch oven or heavy kettle.
2. Fry sausages in a skillet until browned. Put into Dutch oven with chicken. Arrange pineapple, apple, and banana over chicken.
3. For sauce, first prepare chilies (see page 30). (If chilies are not available, substitute chili powder.) Combine chilies, onion, garlic, tomatoes, almonds, cinnamon, and cloves in an electric blender. Blend to a smooth purée.
4. Heat the fat remaining in the skillet in which the sausages were cooked. Add the blended sauce and cook about 5 minutes, stirring constantly. Stir in chicken stock. Season to taste with salt and pepper.
5. Pour sauce over chicken in Dutch oven. Cover and simmer over low heat 1 hour, or until chicken is tender.

*6 to 8 servings*

# Chicken with Rice (Arroz con Pollo)

1 broiler-fryer chicken, (2 to 3 pounds), cut in pieces
¼ cup fat
½ cup chopped onion
1 clove garlic, minced
1 large tomato, chopped
3 cups hot water
1 cup uncooked rice
1 tablespoon minced parsley
2 teaspoons salt
½ teaspoon paprika
¼ teaspoon pepper
¼ teaspoon saffron
1 bay leaf

1. Rinse chicken and pat dry with absorbent paper.
2. Heat fat in a skillet over medium heat. Add onion and garlic; cook until onion is tender. Remove with a slotted spoon; set aside.
3. Put chicken pieces, skin side down, in skillet. Turn to brown pieces on all sides.
4. When chicken is browned, add tomato, onion, water, rice, parsley, and dry seasonings. Cover and cook over low heat about 45 minutes, or until thickest pieces of chicken are tender when pierced with a fork.

*6 to 8 servings*

# Marinated Chicken (Pollo Escabeche)

2 broiler-fryer chickens, cut in serving pieces
1½ cups oil
1 cup cooked sliced carrots
2 large onions, sliced
2 stalks celery, cut in 2-inch pieces
1 clove garlic, minced
⅛ teaspoon thyme
⅛ teaspoon marjoram
1 small bay leaf
12 peppercorns
1 teaspoon salt
3 cups vinegar
Olives, radishes, pickled chilies

1. Brown chicken pieces in hot oil in a skillet. Place browned chicken in a Dutch oven or heavy kettle. Top with carrots, onions, celery, garlic, thyme, marjoram, bay leaf, peppercorns, and salt. Pour vinegar over all.
2. Simmer over low heat until chicken is tender (about 30 to 45 minutes).
3. Remove from heat and let cool to room temperature. Place in refrigerator and chill for at least 1 hour.
4. Garnish with olives, radishes, and chilies.

*8 to 10 servings*

# Green Chicken (Pollo Verde)

1 medium onion, coarsely chopped
1 clove garlic, peeled
1 cup (small can) salsa verde mexicana (Mexican green tomato sauce)
¼ cup (lightly filled) fresh parsley
1 teaspoon salt
¼ teaspoon pepper
2 frying chickens, cut in serving pieces

1. Put onion, garlic, salsa verde, and parsley into an electric blender. Blend until liquefied. Stir in salt and pepper.
2. Rinse chicken pieces and pat dry; arrange pieces in a heavy skillet. Pour green sauce over chicken. Cover; bring to boiling. Cook over low heat until chicken is tender, about 1 hour.

*6 servings*

# Spiced Fruited Chicken

1½ teaspoons salt
¼ teaspoon pepper
¼ teaspoon cinnamon
¼ teaspoon cloves
 2 cloves garlic, minced
 2 frying chickens, cut in serving
     pieces
¼ cup oil
½ cup chopped onion
½ cup raisins
½ cup crushed pineapple
 2 cups orange juice
½ cup dry sherry

1. Combine salt, pepper, cinnamon, cloves, and garlic. Rub into chicken pieces.
2. Heat oil in a heavy skillet. Brown chicken in hot oil. Place browned chicken in a Dutch oven or heavy saucepot.
3. Cook onion in remaining oil in skillet until soft (about 5 minutes).
4. Add onion to chicken along with raisins, pineapple, and orange juice. Add water, if needed, to just cover chicken. Bring to boiling, reduce heat, cover, and cook until chicken is tender (about 1 hour). Add sherry and cook about 5 minutes longer to blend flavors.

*6 to 8 servings*

# Chicken and Mushrooms in Sour Cream Sauce

 2 frying chickens, cut in serving
     pieces
¼ cup oil
 1 pound fresh mushrooms,
     cleaned and sliced
 2 cups canned tomatoes with juice
     (16-ounce can)
 2 canned green chilies, seeded
½ cup chopped onion
 1 clove garlic, minced
 1 cup chicken stock (or water plus
     chicken bouillon cube)
1½ teaspoons salt
 1 cup dairy sour cream

1. Brown chicken pieces in hot oil in a large skillet. Place chicken in Dutch oven or heavy saucepot.
2. Sauté mushrooms in oil remaining in skillet; spoon mushrooms over chicken.
3. Combine tomatoes, chilies, onion, and garlic in an electric blender and blend to a purée (if amount is too large for blender container, blend in two portions).
4. Pour purée into fat remaining in skillet in which chicken and mushrooms were cooked; bring to boiling and cook about 5 minutes. Stir in chicken stock and salt.
5. Pour sauce over chicken and mushrooms in Dutch oven. Cover and cook over low heat until chicken is tender (about 1 hour).
6. Just before serving, stir in sour cream and heat through, but do not boil.

*6 to 8 servings*

The most famous of all mole sauces is probably this one for Mole Poblano which calls for unsweetened chocolate. There are many other Mexican mole sauces, as well. For the word *mole* comes from the Nahuatl Indian word *molli* meaning a sauce made with chili. Most mole sauces are quite *picante* (chili-hot), sometimes too much so for North American palates. Most also call for using several different types of chilies, which often are difficult to obtain in the United States. The simplest way to prepare a very good mole sauce in the United States is to start with a canned or bottled mole paste, which you then dilute with tomato sauce and water. Many Mexican cooks do the same, for preparation of all the chilies plus the many ingredients called for is a time-consuming process. Here we give recipes for making Mole Poblano both ways.

# Chicken or Turkey Mole Poblano I *(with canned mole sauce)*

1 jar (8 ounces) mole poblano paste
1 cup canned tomato sauce
1 cup chicken stock or water
   Sugar and salt
3 cups diced cooked chicken or
   turkey

1. Blend mole paste, tomato sauce, and stock in a large saucepan. Heat to boiling; add sugar and salt to taste. Reduce heat. Stir in chicken. Simmer about 10 to 15 minutes, stirring occasionally, to blend flavors.
2. To use as a tamale filling, the sauce must be fairly thick, so may be simmered until of desired consistency. Then spoon poultry pieces and sauce onto tamale dough spread on corn husk; use leftover sauce to serve over cooked tamales.
3. Or, Chicken or Turkey Mole Poblano may be served over hot rice.

*About 4 cups filling (enough for*
*3½ dozen tamales)*

# Chicken or Turkey Mole Poblano II *(from basic ingredients)*

6 ancho chilies, fresh or dried
2 cups (16-ounce can) cooked
   tomatoes
1 large onion, coarsely chopped
1 clove garlic, peeled
½ cup salted peanuts or ½ cup
   peanut butter
1 tortilla or 1 piece of toast, torn in
   pieces
⅓ cup raisins
2 tablespoons sesame seed
¼ cup oil
1 tablespoon sugar
¼ teaspoon anise
¼ teaspoon cinnamon
¼ teaspoon cloves
¼ teaspoon coriander
¼ teaspoon cumin (comino)
1 cup chicken or turkey stock
1 ounce (1 square) unsweetened
   chocolate
   Salt and pepper
3 cups diced cooked chicken or
   turkey

1. Prepare chilies (see page 30). Combine with tomatoes, onion, garlic, peanuts, tortilla, raisins, and sesame seed. Put a small amount at a time into an electric blender and blend to make a thick purée.
2. Heat oil in a large skillet. Add the purée and cook, stirring constantly, about 5 minutes. Stir in sugar, anise, cinnamon, cloves, coriander, cumin, and stock. Bring to boiling, reduce heat, and simmer. Add chocolate and continue simmering, stirring constantly, until chocolate is melted and blended into sauce. Add salt and pepper to taste. Stir in chicken pieces and simmer about 10 minutes.
3. To use as a tamale filling, the sauce must be fairly thick, so it may be simmered until desired consistency is reached. Then spoon poultry pieces and a little sauce onto tamale dough spread on a corn husk. Use leftover sauce to serve over cooked tamales.
4. Or, Chicken or Turkey Mole Poblano may be served over hot rice.

*About 4 cups filling (enough for*
*3½ dozen tamales)*

# Piquant Chicken

1 frying chicken, cut in serving
    pieces
  Butter or margarine
6 limes or 4 lemons, sliced as
    thinly as possible
  Salt and pepper

1. Brown chicken pieces in butter in a skillet.
2. Place chicken in an ovenproof casserole. Cover completely with lime or lemon slices. Sprinkle with salt and pepper. Cover tightly with foil.
3. Bake at 325°F about 1¼ hours, or until chicken is tender.
4. Serve plain or with Red Chili Sauce (page 30).

*4 servings*

# Stuffed Turkey

1 turkey (12 to 16 pounds)
  Salt and pepper
  Juice of 1 lemon
  Stuffing (see below)
  Melted butter
*Gravy:*
  Flour
  Chicken broth
  White wine
  Salt and pepper

1. Clean turkey. Sprinkle inside and out with salt and pepper, then drizzle with lemon juice.
2. Spoon desired amount of stuffing into cavities of turkey. Secure openings with skewers and twine.
3. Put turkey, breast side up, on a rack in a shallow roasting pan. Cover bird with a double thickness of cheesecloth soaked in butter.
4. Roast in a 325°F oven 4½ to 5½ hours, or until done (180°F to 185°F on a meat thermometer inserted in inside thigh muscle or thickest part of breast); baste with drippings several times during roasting.
5. For gravy, stir a small amount of flour with pan drippings. Cook until bubbly. Stir in equal parts of broth and wine. Season to taste with salt and pepper.
6. Put turkey on a platter and garnish with **watercress.** Accompany with gravy.

*12 to 16 servings*

# Stuffing

5 slices bacon, diced
1 onion, chopped
1 clove garlic, minced
3 pounds ground pork loin
½ cup tomato purée
¾ cup blanched almonds, chopped
½ cup ripe olives, coarsely chopped
6 jalapeño chilies, seeded and
    chopped
3 carrots, pared and sliced
3 bananas, peeled and sliced
3 apples, pared, cored, and diced
¾ cup raisins
2 teaspoons sugar
  Salt and pepper
  Cinnamon

1. Fry bacon until brown in a large skillet. Remove bacon from fat; reserve. Brown onion and garlic in fat in skillet, then brown meat. Discard excess fat.
2. Add tomato purée, almonds, olives, chilies, carrots, fruit, sugar, and salt, pepper, and cinnamon to taste; mix well. Cook several minutes. Mix in bacon. Cool before stuffing turkey.

# Red Snapper Veracruz Style

*Red Snapper Veracruz Style is one of Mexico's famous fish entrées. The sauce of tomatoes, onion, olives, and capers is also frequently used with haddock, and is equally delicious with other similar fish.*

¼ cup olive oil
1 cup chopped onion
1 clove garlic, minced
2 cups (16-ounce can) tomatoes
    with liquid
1 teaspoon salt
¼ teaspoon pepper
2 pounds red snapper fillets
¼ cup sliced pimento-stuffed olives
2 tablespoons capers
    Lemon wedges

1. Heat oil in a large skillet. Cook onion and garlic in hot oil until onion is soft, about 5 minutes. Add tomatoes, salt, and pepper and cook about 5 minutes to blend flavors; slightly chop tomatoes as they cook.
2. Arrange red snapper fillets in a 3-quart baking dish. Pour sauce over fish. Sprinkle with olives and capers.
3. Bake at 350°F 25 to 30 minutes, or until fish can be flaked easily with a fork. Serve with lemon wedges.

*About 6 servings*

# Drunken Fish

*A number of traditional Mexican recipes call for "drunken" sauce—another example of the penchant for humorous food names. They may use dry white or red wine, tequila, or pulque (another alcoholic beverage made from the maguey cactus, like tequila). This recipe for Drunken Fish calls for dry red wine in a chili-tomato sauce.*

1 whole red snapper or similar
    fish, or 5 pounds fish fillets
    Flour, seasoned with salt and
    pepper
¼ cup oil
1 cup chopped onion
1 clove garlic, minced
6 fresh or dried ancho chilies
1½ cups canned tomatoes
2 tablespoons dried parsley
½ teaspoon oregano
½ teaspoon cumin (comino)
    Salt and pepper
2 cups dry red wine
2 tablespoons capers

1. Dredge the fish with seasoned flour. Heat oil in a large skillet and brown fish on both sides. Remove fish from skillet and place in a shallow baking dish.
2. Add onion and garlic to oil remaining in skillet and cook until onion is soft, about 5 minutes.
3. Prepare chilies (see page 30); place in an electric blender and blend to a thick purée. Add to onion and garlic in skillet and cook about 5 minutes. Add tomatoes, parsley, oregano, and cumin. Bring to boiling, stirring constantly. Season to taste with salt and pepper. Stir in red wine and mix well.
4. Pour sauce over fish in baking dish.
5. Bake at 400°F about 30 minutes, or until fish flakes easily. Garnish with capers and serve.

*6 to 8 servings*

# Codfish for Christmas

1 pound salted codfish (1 piece)
2 small onions, peeled
  Salt and pepper
3 medium (1 pound) tomatoes, peeled, seeded, and cut in pieces
2 cloves garlic, peeled
3 tablespoons oil
5 pickled chilies, seeded and cut in strips
3 canned pimentos, cut in strips
½ cup pimento-stuffed olives
1 tablespoon chopped parsley

1. Soak codfish several hours in cold water; change water several times.
2. Drain codfish and put into a saucepan; add 1 onion and water to cover. Bring to simmering, cover, and cook gently about 15 minutes, or until fish flakes easily when tested with a fork. Drain. Season with salt and pepper.
3. Meanwhile, purée tomatoes, remaining onion (cut in quarters), and garlic in an electric blender.
4. Heat oil in a skillet and add the red sauce. Cook until thicker, stirring occasionally. Mix in chili and pimento strips.
5. To serve, put the codfish on a platter, pour the sauce over it, and garnish with whole olives and parsley. Accompany with **cooked rice.**

*About 4 servings*

# Pickled Tuna *(Atún en Escabeche)*

*This is an adaptation of a Mexican favorite, Escabeche. The word escabeche means pickled, and usually refers to one of the popular recipes for chilled pickled fish. Normally a mild-flavored white fish is called for, but in this recipe canned tuna is prepared "en escabeche." Serve as an appetizer, as Escabeche is usually served in Mexico, or as a luncheon salad.*

2 cans (6½ to 7 ounces each) tuna, drained
  Juice of 2 limes or 1 lemon
¼ cup oil
1 medium onion, thinly sliced (about ½ cup)
2 canned jalapeño chilies, seeded and cut in thin strips
1 clove garlic, minced
½ teaspoon oregano
½ teaspoon cumin (comino)
¾ cup wine or cider vinegar
  Lettuce leaves
  Sliced pimento-stuffed olives

1. Put tuna into a jar or bowl with lid; flake with fork. Pour lime juice over fish and let stand while preparing pickling mixture.
2. Heat oil in skillet. Add onion, chilies, and garlic; cook about 5 minutes, until onion is soft. Stir in oregano and cumin, then stir in vinegar. Bring to boiling.
3. Pour sauce over fish and stir until well coated.
4. Cover and refrigerate several hours. Serve on lettuce garnished with olive slices.

*6 servings*

# Fish Campeche Style

1 pound fish fillets, fresh or frozen
½ cup orange juice
1 can (6 ounces) tomato paste
1 cup water
¼ cup chopped onion

1. Place fish fillets in a medium-sized skillet and add water to cover. Add ¼ cup of the orange juice. Bring to boiling, reduce heat, and simmer about 10 minutes, or until fish flakes when tested with a fork. Drain and skin, if necessary. Cut fish into finger-sized pieces. Return to skillet.

1 teaspoon chili powder
Salt and pepper

2. Meanwhile, in a small saucepan, combine remaining orange juice, tomato paste, 1 cup of water, onion, and chili powder. Bring to boiling; season with salt and pepper to taste. Pour over fish fingers. Simmer fish in this sauce until well coated and sauce starts to thicken.

*4 to 6 servings*

Seviche or ceviche (both spellings are often used) appears on the menu of restaurants throughout Mexico. It's a seafood dish, generally served as an appetizer, but sometimes as a light luncheon entrée. The fish is "cooked" by the action of citric acid in lime or lemon juice. Seviche is another food popularly sold at street-side stands in the larger Mexican cities.

## Seviche I

1 pound pompano (or other
    mild-flavored fish fillets)
    Juice of 6 limes (or lemons)
2 medium tomatoes, peeled and
    chopped
2 tablespoons finely chopped onion
1 or 2 canned jalapeño chilies,
    seeded and finely chopped
¼ cup olive oil
1 tablespoon vinegar
¼ teaspoon oregano
    Salt and pepper
    Sliced green olives
    Chopped parsley

1. Wash the fish very well. Cut into small chunks or strips and place in a glass jar or glass bowl with cover. Pour lime juice over fish; cover and refrigerate about 6 hours. (Lime juice will "cook" raw fish until it is white and firm.)
2. At least a half hour before serving, add tomato, onion, chili, olive oil, vinegar, oregano, and salt and pepper to taste; stir gently until evenly mixed.
3. When ready to serve, garnish with sliced olives and parsley.

*6 servings*

## Seviche II

1 pound fresh firm-fleshed
    boneless white fish
¾ cup lemon juice
1 teaspoon salt
3 canned green chilies, seeded and
    chopped
2 ripe medium tomatoes, peeled,
    seeded, and chopped
2 small onions, thinly sliced
2 teaspoons coriander
⅓ cup olive oil
2 tablespoons vinegar

1. Remove skin from fish; cut into small pieces and put into a deep bowl. Add lemon juice and salt; toss. Cover and refrigerate 1 to 2 hours.
2. Toss gently. Add remaining ingredients; mix thoroughly. Chill.
3. Serve in shells or cocktail glasses and, if desired, garnish with avocado slices.

*About 6 servings*

# Poached Fish with Almonds

*Poached fish garnished with nuts is another seafood entrée. This sauce calls for dry white wine and Mexican green tomato sauce.*

1 cup dry white wine
1 small can salsa verde mexicana (Mexican green tomato sauce)
½ cup chopped onion
1 clove garlic, minced
Salt and pepper
2 pounds fish fillets (halibut, flounder, sole, or other white fish)
½ cup toasted slivered almonds ·
Lemon wedges

1. Combine wine, salsa verde, onion, and garlic in a large skillet. Season with salt and pepper to taste. Bring to boiling, reduce heat, and simmer about 10 to 15 minutes.
2. Place fish fillets in simmering sauce and cook until fish flakes easily with a fork, about 5 to 10 minutes.
3. Transfer fish to a heated platter, spoon some of the sauce over fish, and sprinkle wtih almonds. Serve with lemon wedges.

*About 6 servings*

# Veracruz Style Crab-Filled Fish Rolls

6 fish fillets (such as red snapper or sole), cut into long, thin slices
Juice of 1 lemon or lime
½ cup milk
2 tablespoons olive oil
½ cup chopped onion
1 clove garlic, minced
1 small tomato, peeled and chopped
1 teaspoon minced parsley
1 teaspoon salt
Dash of pepper
¼ pound crab meat, shredded
¼ pound shredded Monterey Jack
1 cup dairy sour cream
1 egg yolk
¼ pound butter or margarine

1. Rinse fish; rub with lemon or lime juice; soak in milk.
2. Meanwhile, heat olive oil in a small skillet. Sauté onion and garlic in oil; add tomato and cook until no longer juicy. Remove from heat and stir in parsley, salt, and pepper. Add crab meat and ⅓ of the cheese and mix well.
3. Remove fish from milk and pat dry with paper towels. Place a small amount of crab meat filling on one end of fillet and roll up, as for a jelly roll. Place fish rolls in one layer in a greased baking dish.
4. Beat sour cream with egg yolk and pour over fish. Dot with butter. Sprinkle remaining cheese over top.
5. Bake at 350°F until golden brown and cheese is melted (about 20 minutes).

*6 servings*

# Shrimp with Red Rice

¼ cup oil
½ cup chopped onion
1 clove garlic, minced
1 medium green pepper, seeded and sliced in ½-inch strips
1 pound shelled green shrimp
1 can (6 ounces) tomato paste
2½ cups water
1 teaspoon salt
¼ teaspoon pepper
¼ teaspoon marjoram
1 cup uncooked rice

1. Heat oil in a large, heavy saucepan. Add onion and garlic and cook until soft (about 5 minutes). Add green pepper and uncooked shrimp and cook until shrimp turn pink.
2. Stir tomato paste, water, and seasonings into shrimp mixture and bring to boiling. Add rice; mix well. Cover and simmer over very low heat until all liquid is absorbed by rice (about 25 to 30 minutes).

*4 to 6 servings*

# Shrimp with Sesame Seed Sauce

½ cup plain pumpkin seed
3 tablespoons sesame seed
1 small clove garlic
2 tablespoons vegetable oil
¾ teaspoon chili powder
¼ teaspoon cinnamon
⅛ teaspoon cloves
¾ cup canned chicken broth
½ teaspoon salt
1½ tablespoons lime juice
1½ pounds hot cooked shelled
    shrimp

1. Combine pumpkin seed, sesame seed, garlic, and oil in a saucepan. Stir and cook over medium heat until sesame seed is light golden brown.
2. Remove from heat and stir in chili powder, cinnamon, and cloves. Turn into an electric blender and grind. Add broth and salt; blend.
3. Turn mixture into a saucepan, mix in lime juice, and heat over low heat, stirring in one direction, until thickened.
4. Arrange hot shrimp on a platter and spoon sauce over it. If desired, garnish with sliced green onion and lime wedges.

*4 servings*

Paella is one of the dishes Mexico has adopted from Spain. There are many versions of this famous dish, which usually contains whatever seafood is most readily available. Here are two delicious versions.

# Paella I

1 cup sliced carrots
1 small onion, sliced
2 bay leaves
1 tablespoon dried parsley
¼ teaspoon pepper
3 cups water
½ cup oil
2 broiler-fryer chickens, cut in
    serving pieces
2 cloves garlic, minced
1 green pepper, cut in thin strips
1 teaspoon crumbled saffron
1 can (12 ounces) clams or 8 to 12
    fresh clams
1½ cups uncooked rice
1 tablespoon salt
2 large tomatoes, peeled and
    chopped
1 can (8 ounces) artichoke hearts
1 pound cooked shrimp, shelled
    and deveined

1. Place carrots, onion, bay leaves, dried parsley, pepper, and water in saucepan; simmer over low heat about 20 minutes, or until carrots are tender.
2. Meanwhile, heat oil in a large Dutch oven or heavy kettle. Brown chicken pieces in oil, a few at a time, removing as they are well browned.
3. In same oil, sauté garlic, pepper strips, and saffron. Return chicken pieces to Dutch oven. Drain liquid from clams and add enough of this liquid to vegetable liquid to make 3 cups. Pour over chicken in Dutch oven. Bring to simmering and gradually stir in rice and salt.
4. Bake at 350°F 1 hour.
5. During last part of baking, prepare clams by cutting in half; chop tomatoes; cut artichoke hearts into quarters vertically. Add clams, tomatoes, shrimp, and artichoke hearts to chicken-rice mixture, and mix in carefully. Return to oven for 10 to 15 minutes more, or until heated through. Serve hot.

*8 to 10 servings*

# Paella II

1 cup olive oil or vegetable oil
1 broiler-fryer chicken (2 pounds), cut in pieces
½ cup diced boiled ham or smoky sausage
1 tablespoon minced onion
2 cloves garlic, minced
2 ripe tomatoes, peeled and coarsely chopped
1½ teaspoons salt
1½ pounds fresh shrimp, shelled and deveined
12 small clams in shells, scrubbed
2 cups uncooked rice
1 quart hot water
1 cup fresh or frozen green peas
¼ cup coarsely chopped parsley
Few shreds saffron
1 rock lobster tail, cooked and meat cut in pieces
1 can or jar (7 ounces) whole pimentos

1. Heat oil in paellera or large skillet; cook chicken and ham about 10 minutes, turning chicken to brown on all sides. Add onion and garlic and cook 2 minutes. Add tomatoes, salt, shrimp, and clams; cover and cook 5 to 10 minutes, or until clam shells open. Remove clams and keep warm.
2. Add rice, water, peas, parsley, and saffron; mix well. Cover and cook, stirring occasionally, 25 minutes, or until rice is just tender. Mix in lobster, half of pimento, and the reserved clams in shells; heat until very hot. Serve garnished with remaining pimento.

*8 to 10 servings*

# Ranch-Style Eggs (Huevos Rancheros)

2 tablespoons oil
¼ cup chopped onion
1 clove garlic, minced
2 cups canned tomatoes with juice (16-ounce can), chopped
1 cup canned tomato sauce
1 teaspoon salt
1 teaspoon chili powder
½ teaspoon sugar
¼ teaspoon pepper
6 to 8 eggs
Oil for frying
6 to 8 tortillas

1. For sauce, heat 2 tablespoons oil in a 10-inch skillet. Add onion and garlic and cook until onion is soft, about 5 minutes. Add tomatoes, tomato sauce, salt, chili powder, sugar, and pepper; stir thoroughly and bring to boiling. Reduce heat and simmer about 10 minutes, stirring occasionally.
2. Break eggs carefully into simmering sauce. Poach 3 to 4 minutes, or until yolks are just starting to set; if desired, occasionally spoon a little sauce over eggs as they cook. Or eggs can be fried in oil.
3. Meanwhile, heat about ¼-inch oil in another skillet. Fry tortillas in hot oil until either limp or crisp, turning to brown both sides; drain on absorbent paper.
4. To serve, place each warm tortilla on a plate, spoon some sauce over tortilla, and top with poached egg.

*6 to 8 servings*

*Note:* Canned Mexican salsa casera, if available in your area, and tomato sauce in equal parts may be substituted for the sauce recipe.

# Scrambled Eggs Mexicana

½ cup Fresh Tomato Sauce (see page 20), or canned salsa casera or enchilada sauce
6 to 8 eggs
⅓ cup cream
½ teaspoon salt
4 to 6 soft corn tortillas
½ cup shredded Monterey Jack or mild Cheddar cheese

1. Heat tomato sauce in a lightly buttered skillet. If using fresh tomato sauce, cook about 5 minutes until onion is soft.
2. Beat eggs with cream and salt. Pour egg mixture into hot sauce and cook over medium heat, stirring constantly, until eggs are set.
3. Meanwhile, heat tortillas in an ungreased medium-hot skillet or griddle, turning frequently.
4. To serve, place a hot soft tortilla on plate and spoon eggs on top. Sprinkle with cheese. Serve immediately.

*4 to 6 servings*

# Scrambled Eggs with Tomato

2 teaspoons minced onion
1 tablespoon vegetable oil
1 fresh tomato, peeled, seeded, and chopped
2 tablespoons chopped green pepper
1 teaspoon salt
3 drops Tabasco
6 eggs

1. Sauté onion in oil in a skillet. Add tomato, green pepper, salt, and Tabasco; mix well. Cook 3 to 5 minutes.
2. Add eggs, one at a time, to skillet and mix into sauce. Cook until eggs are set.
3. Serve immediately on heated **tortillas.**

*4 servings*

# Eggs Scrambled with Chorizo and Tomatoes

½ pound Chorizo Filling (see page 18)
1 cup diced tomatoes (fresh or canned)
½ teaspoon salt
8 eggs, beaten
Refried Beans (page 28)

1. Crumble chorizo filling into a skillet; brown well. Stir in tomatoes and salt, then add beaten eggs, Cook over low heat, stirring frequently, until eggs are set.
2. Serve immediately accompanied with refried beans.

*4 to 6 servings*

# Eggs Chilaquiles

2 tablespoons butter or margarine
4 corn tortillas, sliced into ½-inch strips
1 cup chopped tomatoes (fresh or canned)
1 tablespoon instant minced onion
4 eggs, slightly beaten
½ teaspoon salt
⅛ teaspoon pepper
Dash Tabasco
Parmesan cheese

1. Melt butter in a large skillet. Fry tortilla strips in hot butter. Stir in tomatoes and instant onion and heat to boiling. Stir in eggs, salt, pepper, and Tabasco and cook until eggs are set, stirring frequently.
2. Serve at once, topped with Parmesan cheese.

*4 servings*

# Queso Fundido

*The name of this dish translates literally to "melted cheese" and that's exactly what it is—a sort of simplified Mexican version of cheese fondue. Queso Fundido appears frequently on the menus of Mexican restaurants, and usually is served as an appetizer. At home it makes a great luncheon main dish or a fun snack.*

**1 pound Monterey Jack**
**1 dozen warm soft corn tortillas**
   **Fresh Tomato Sauce (see page 20)**

1. Slice cheese into 4 individual or 1 large flat ovenproof ramekin.
2. Place in a 350°F oven. Heat until cheese melts and starts to bubble.
3. Serve at once accompanied with tortillas and sauce. To eat, cut sections of hot cheese and fold inside tortillas; eat plain or with sauce.

*4 servings*

The crisp-crusted, soft-centered Mexican bread rolls, called "bolillos," closely resemble the texture of French bread. In Mexican restaurants these rolls are often served stuffed with mild-flavored cheese and perhaps a bit of meat, then doused in spicy sauce. Thus served they are dubbed "lonches"—a takeoff of the English word "lunch"? Perhaps. Here's a somewhat Americanized version which will make a delicious light lunch or heavy snack, by whatever name it's called.

# Hot Cheese and Bacon Sandwiches

**6 large hard rolls or 1 long loaf**
   **French bread, cut in 6**
   **sections**
**½ pound Monterey Jack, sliced**
**6 slices bacon, cooked crisp**
**1½ cups canned enchilada sauce or**
   **Red Chili Sauce (page 30)**

1. Split rolls or bread sections in half horizontally. Fill generously with cheese and top cheese with bacon strip. Close rolls to form sandwiches and place on a baking sheet.
2. Heat in a 350°F oven 5 to 10 minutes, or until rolls are hot and cheese melted.
3. Meanwhile, heat sauce to bubbling.
4. To serve, place each filled roll in flat soup dish and ladle ¼ cup sauce over top.

*6 servings*

# ACCOMPANIMENTS

## SOUPS

Soups play an important role in Mexican meals. In the traditional midday *comida* menu the entrée is always preceded by a soup. This may vary from the familiar hot meat, chicken, fish, or vegetable type to a cold soup of chopped raw vegetables, which is most unusual indeed. Most Mexican soups start with meat or poultry stock, which the good Mexican cook keeps on hand in her refrigerator or freezer. However, you may prefer to substitute canned broth or make bouillon with water plus bouillon cubes.

Much confusion occurs among visitors to Mexico over that unusually named group of dishes called "dry soups." These are not really soups at all, as we think of them, but rather casserole-like dishes based on pasta, rice, or tortillas. In the traditional, large Mexican *comida* both types will be included, one "wet" and the other "dry." The latter is served as a second or third course, much in the same manner as the Italians serve pastas. No one seems quite sure how dry soups got their name. But perhaps it is because they start with meat or poultry stock in which the starchy food is cooked until all the liquid is absorbed. We North Americans might be likely to serve one of the dry soups as a luncheon or supper main dish. Or, they make excellent meat accompaniments, taking the place of our traditional potatoes.

## *Chicken Stock*

1 **large stewing chicken, cut in**
   **serving pieces**
4 **quarts water**
1 **large onion, chopped**
1 **stalk celery, sliced**
1 **carrot, pared and sliced**
1 **clove garlic, minced**
2 **teaspoons salt**
¼ **teaspoon pepper**

1. Rinse chicken and place in large kettle. Cover with the water. Bring to boiling. Add all remaining ingredients. Cover kettle, reduce heat, and simmer until chicken is tender (about 2 hours).
2. Cool; remove chicken and use in other recipes calling for cooked chicken. Strain broth, skim fat, and refrigerate broth until ready to use. (Or the broth, with or without vegetables, may be used as a simple soup.)

*About 3 quarts stock*

# Beef Stock

2 pounds beef pot roast or brisket
   or beef for stew
2 pounds beef short ribs
1 marrow bone
4 quarts water
1 large onion, chopped
1 stalk celery, sliced
2 carrots, pared and sliced
1 cup canned tomatoes
1 clove garlic, minced
2 teaspoons salt
¼ teaspoon pepper
1 bay leaf (optional)

1. Put meats and bone into a large kettle. Cover with the water. Bring to boiling. Add all remaining ingredients. Cover kettle, reduce heat, and simmer until meat is tender (3 to 4 hours).
2. Skim fat from broth. Cool, remove meat, and use in recipes such as Picadillo (page 17). Strain broth and refrigerate until ready to use. (Or the broth, with or without vegetables, may be used as a simple soup.)

*About 3 quarts stock*

# Tortilla Soup

*This is a light soup, good for a first course at dinner, and is one use for stale tortillas.*

2 quarts chicken or beef stock,
   canned consommé, or water
   plus bouillon cubes
½ cup chopped onion
1 cup canned tomato sauce or
   purée
1 teaspoon salt
¼ teaspoon pepper
6 to 8 stale tortillas
   Oil for frying
1½ cups shredded Monterey Jack or
   mild Cheddar cheese
   (optional)

1. Heat stock with onion to boiling. Reduce heat and simmer about 5 minutes. Stir in tomato sauce, salt, and pepper; simmer about 5 minutes.
2. Meanwhile, cut tortillas into ½-inch strips and fry in hot oil until crisp; drain on absorbent paper.
3. To serve soup, place a handful of crisp tortilla strips in soup bowl and ladle soup on top. Sprinkle with cheese, if desired.

*About 2 quarts soup*

# Pozole

*This hearty soup comes from Guadalajara, capital of the Mexican state of Jalisco. The everyday variety calls for pork head as the only meat. This richer version uses pork hocks and loin as well as chicken, and obviously is a meal in itself. Pozole is always served with a variety of crisp vegetable garnishes which are sprinkled on top of the hot soup at the diner's discretion.*

2 pork hocks, split in two or three
   pieces each
1 large onion, sliced
2 cloves garlic, minced

1. Put split pork hocks, onion, and garlic into a kettle, cover with water, and cook until almost tender (about 3 hours).
2. Add chicken and pork loin and cook 45 minutes, or until chicken is almost tender.

Water
1 stewing chicken, cut in serving
    pieces
1 pound pork loin, boneless, cut in
    1-inch chunks
2 cups canned hominy or canned
    garbanzos
1 tablespoon salt
½ teaspoon pepper
1 cup sliced crisp radishes
1 cup shredded cabbage
1 cup shredded lettuce
½ cup chopped green onions
    Lime or lemon wedges

3. Add hominy, salt, and pepper. Cook about 15 minutes, or until all meat is tender.
4. Remove pork hocks and chicken from soup. Remove meat from bones and return meat to soup.
5. Serve in large soup bowls. Accompany with a relish tray offering the radishes, cabbage, lettuce, green onions, and lime or lemon wedges as garnishes.

*8 to 10 servings*

## Fish Soup

1 head and bones from large fish,
    such as red snapper
1 bay leaf
1 onion, coarsely chopped
2 stalks celery
1½ quarts water
2 cups (16-ounce can) tomatoes
    with juice
1 cup sliced carrots
1 cup diced pared potatoes
1 or 2 diced jalapeño chilies
1 cup dry sherry
1 pound diced, boneless fillets of
    white fish, or deveined
    shrimp
½ teaspoon garlic salt
½ teaspoon marjoram
    Salt and pepper

1. Put fish head and bones into a kettle with bay leaf, onion, celery, and water. Boil 15 minutes. Remove from heat and strain liquid, returning it to kettle. Discard solids.
2. Add tomatoes, carrots, potatoes, and chilies to liquid in kettle. Simmer until carrots and potatoes are almost tender (about 15 minutes).
3. Add sherry, diced fish, garlic salt, marjoram, and salt and pepper to taste to kettle. Cook about 5 minutes, or until fish flakes easily with fork.

*2½ to 3 quarts soup*

## Soup Mexicana

1 chicken breast
1½ quarts chicken broth
2 onions, chopped
1 tablespoon butter or margarine
1½ teaspoons grated onion
2 cups chopped zucchini
1 cup drained canned whole
    kernel corn
⅓ cup tomato purée
2 ounces cream cheese, cut in
    small cubes
2 avocados, sliced

1. Combine chicken breast, broth, and onion in a large saucepan. Cover, bring to boiling, reduce heat, and cook 30 minutes, or until chicken is tender.
2. Remove chicken; dice and set aside. Reserve broth.
3. Heat butter and grated onion in a large saucepan; stir in zucchini and corn. Cook about 5 minutes, stirring occasionally. Mix in broth and tomato purée. Cover and simmer about 20 minutes.
4. Just before serving, mix in diced chicken, cream cheese, and avocado slices.

*6 to 8 servings*

*Note:* Any remaining soup may be stored, covered, in refrigerator.

# Corn Soup I

½ cup finely chopped onion
2 tablespoons butter
1 quart beef stock or canned beef broth
2½ cups cooked whole kernel golden corn
3 tomatoes, peeled, halved, and seeded
Salt and pepper
1 cup whipping cream
Dairy sour cream

1. Cook onion in butter in a saucepan until onion is soft.
2. Put onion and a small amount of stock into an electric blender. Add 2 cups corn and tomato halves; blend until smooth.
3. Turn purée into saucepan and mix in remaining stock. Season to taste with salt and pepper. Bring to boiling, reduce heat, and cook 5 minutes. Add cream gradually, stirring constantly. Heat thoroughly, but do not boil.
4. Garnish soup with dollops of sour cream and remaining corn.

*6 to 8 servings*

# Corn Soup II

2 tablespoons butter or margarine
½ cup chopped onion
2 cups (17-ounce can) cream-style corn
1 cup canned tomato sauce
3 cups chicken stock, canned chicken broth, or 3 cups water plus 3 chicken bouillon cubes
1 cup cream
Salt and pepper

1. Melt butter in a large saucepan. Add onion and cook until soft. Add corn, tomato sauce, and stock. Bring to boiling, reduce heat, and simmer about 10 minutes to blend flavors, stirring frequently.
2. Remove from heat and stir in cream. Season to taste with salt and pepper. Serve hot.

*6 to 8 servings*

# Avocado Soup

4 fully ripe avocados, peeled and pitted
3 cups cold chicken broth
2 teaspoons lime juice
½ teaspoon salt
⅛ teaspoon garlic powder
2 cups chilled cream

1. Put all ingredients except cream into an electric blender container. Cover and blend until smooth. Mix with the cream and chill thoroughly.
2. Serve with **lemon slices** or garnish as desired.

*6 servings*

# Bean Soup

2 cups cooked Basic Mexican Beans (page 27), or canned kidney beans with liquid
1 cup beef stock, canned beef broth, or 1 cup water plus 1 beef bouillon cube
1 cup cooked tomatoes with liquid
1 clove garlic, minced
½ teaspoon oregano
½ teaspoon chili powder
Salt and pepper

1. Put beans into a large saucepan. Mash with a potato masher, leaving some large pieces. Add meat stock, tomatoes, garlic, oregano, and chili powder. Bring to boiling, reduce heat, and simmer about 10 minutes, stirring frequently.
2. Add salt and pepper to taste. Serve hot.

*About 1 quart soup*

# Black Bean Soup

1 pound dried black beans, washed
2 quarts boiling water
2 tablespoons salt
5 cloves garlic
1½ teaspoons cumin (comino)
1½ teaspoons oregano
2 tablespoons white vinegar
10 tablespoons olive oil
½ pound onions, peeled and chopped
½ pound green peppers, trimmed and chopped

1. Put beans into a large, heavy saucepot or Dutch oven and add boiling water; boil rapidly 2 minutes. Cover tightly, remove from heat, and set aside 1 hour. Add salt to beans and liquid; bring to boiling and simmer, covered, until beans are soft, about 2 hours.
2. Put the garlic, cumin, oregano, and vinegar into a mortar and crush to a paste.
3. Heat olive oil in a large skillet. Mix in onion and green pepper and fry until onion is browned, stirring occasionally. Thoroughly blend in the paste, then stir the skillet mixture into the beans. Cook over low heat until ready to serve.
4. Meanwhile, mix a small portion of **cooked rice, minced onion, olive oil,** and **vinegar** in a bowl; set aside to marinate. Add a soup spoon of rice mixture to each serving of soup.

*About 2 quarts soup*

# Gazpacho

*Gazpacho is a refreshing cold soup made with fresh, raw vegetables. It is so filled with vegetable chunks that it seems almost like a salad. Serve it very well chilled, and keep bowls over ice, or place an ice cube in each bowl just as it is served.*

1 clove garlic
2 cups chopped peeled fresh tomatoes
1 large cucumber, pared and chopped
½ cup diced green pepper
½ cup chopped onion
1 cup tomato juice
3 tablespoons olive oil
2 tablespoons vinegar
Salt and pepper
Dash Tabasco
½ cup crisp croutons

1. Cut garlic in half and rub onto bottom and sides of a large bowl. Add tomatoes, cucumber, green pepper, onion, tomato juice, olive oil, and vinegar to bowl and stir until evenly mixed. Season to taste with salt, pepper, and Tabasco.
2. Chill in refrigerator at least 1 hour before serving.
3. Serve soup in chilled bowls. Top each serving with a few croutons.

*8 to 10 servings*

# Avocado Yogurt Soup

*Here is another cold soup, very different from Gazpacho, and perfect as a warm-weather meal appetizer.*

1 cup avocado pulp (2 to 3 avocados, depending on size)
⅔ cup unsweetened yogurt
⅔ cup beef stock, or bouillon made with ⅔ cup water and 1 bouillon cube, then chilled
1 tablespoon lemon juice
1 teaspoon onion juice or grated onion
½ teaspoon salt
Dash Tabasco

1. Put avocado pulp and yogurt into an electric blender and blend until evenly mixed. Adding gradually, blend in beef stock, lemon juice, onion juice, salt, and Tabasco. Chill well.
2. Serve soup in chilled bowls.

*4 to 6 servings*

# Cream-Style Gazpacho with Avocado

4 hard-cooked eggs
¼ cup oil
1 tablespoon prepared mustard
1 tablespoon Worcestershire sauce
¼ cup lemon juice
1 teaspoon garlic salt
¼ teaspoon pepper
5 fresh medium tomatoes
1 large cucumber
1 medium onion
1 ripe avocado
1 cup dairy sour cream

1. Peel eggs; slice in half and remove yolks; set whites aside. Put egg yolks into a small bowl and mash with fork; blend in oil until of paste consistency. Blend in mustard, Worcestershire sauce, lemon juice, garlic salt, and pepper. Set aside.

2. Peel tomatoes; set aside one for garnish; coarsely chop remaining 4 and put into an electric blender. Pare and seed cucumber. Set aside ¼ as garnish; chop remaining ¾ and place in blender with tomatoes. Peel, coarsely chop, and add onion to blender. Peel avocado and place half in blender with vegetables. Reserve remaining half for garnish. Blend contents of blender until smooth. Add egg yolk mixture and blend until thoroughly mixed. Add sour cream gradually, blending well.

3. Pour soup into container with cover.

4. Chop remaining tomato, cucumber, and hard-cooked egg whites and add to soup. Slice remaining avocado half thinly and add to soup. Stir in lightly. Cover and refrigerate until well chilled.

*About 6 servings*

# Chili con Carne

*Chili con Carne is not, strictly speaking, an authentic Mexican soup. However, it is so associated with Mexican food in the minds of most North Americans, and besides, is so delicious, that a recipe is included here.*

1½ pounds ground beef
1 large onion, chopped
1 clove garlic, minced
4 cups (two 16-ounce cans) cooked tomatoes
2 cups (one 15-ounce can) red kidney beans
1 tablespoon chili powder
2 teaspoons salt
¼ teaspoon pepper

1. Cook ground beef in a large skillet, stirring until crumbled into small pieces and well browned.

2. Add onion and garlic to meat; cook about 5 minutes, stirring frequently.

3. Add tomatoes to skillet and chop into bite-size chunks. Stir in kidney beans, chili powder, salt, and pepper. Reduce heat to simmering and cook, stirring occasionally, about 30 minutes.

*6 to 8 servings*

# Meatball Soup

**Meatballs:**
- 1½ pounds ground beef
- ½ pound ground pork
- 1 egg, beaten
- 2 slices bread
- ¼ cup milk
- 1½ teaspoons salt
- ¼ teaspoon pepper
- 1 clove garlic, minced

**Soup:**
- 2½ quarts water
- 1 cup mint leaves
- 2 tablespoons oil
- ¼ cup chopped onion
- 1 cup tomato paste
- ½ teaspoon chili powder
- Salt and pepper

1. For meatballs, combine beef, pork, and beaten egg.
2. Shred bread and soak in milk; add to meat mixture; add salt, pepper, and garlic and mix well. Form into 1½-inch balls.
3. For the soup, heat water in a large kettle; add mint leaves. Drop meatballs into simmering liquid, a few at a time to keep water boiling. Cook until meatballs are cooked through (about 15 minutes).
4. While meatballs are simmering, heat oil in a saucepan; add onion and cook until soft (about 5 minutes). Stir in tomato paste and heat to boiling.
5. Stir tomato-onion mixture and chili powder into soup with meatballs. Season to taste with salt and pepper. Heat about 5 minutes longer to blend flavors.

*6 to 8 servings*

# Quick Tomato-Fish Stew

- 3 tablespoons oil
- ½ cup chopped onion
- 1 clove garlic, minced
- 2 cups canned tomatoes with juice (16-ounce can)
- 2 cups cooked garbanzos, drained (16-ounce can)
- ½ pound boned white fish, flaked
- Salt and pepper

1. Heat oil in a kettle. Add onion and garlic and cook until soft (about 5 minutes). Add tomatoes and garbanzos and bring to boiling. Add flaked fish, reduce heat, and cook about 15 minutes longer. Season to taste with salt and pepper.
2. Serve with **pickled hot chilies.**

*6 to 8 servings*

# Spinach-Ball Soup

*Here is another example of the Mexican way with unusual soups. The little deep-fried spinach-wrapped balls give the soup its name. They're so delicious by themselves that you might like to serve them as a hot appetizer.*

**Spinach Balls:**
- 2 pounds fresh spinach
- ½ cup cooked cubed ham
- ½ cup cubed Cheddar cheese
- 3 eggs, separated
- 1 tablespoon flour
- Dash salt
- Oil for deep frying

**Soup:**
- 2 tablespoons oil
- ½ cup chopped onion
- 1 clove garlic, minced
- 1 can (6 ounces) tomato paste
- 3 cups chicken or meat stock or canned bouillon
- Salt and pepper

1. For spinach balls, wash spinach well and remove hard stalks. Steam until tender, in a small amount of boiling salted water in a large saucepot. Drain. Cool slightly and form into balls about 1¼ inches in diameter. Push a piece of ham or cheese into center of each ball.
2. Beat egg whites until stiff; gradually beat in yolks, flour, and salt. Coat spinach balls with egg batter and fry one layer of balls at a time in hot oil until lightly browned.
3. Meanwhile, prepare soup. Heat 2 tablespoons oil in a large kettle. Add onion and garlic and cook until soft (about 5 minutes). Stir in tomato paste and stock. Heat to boiling, reduce heat, and simmer gently about 15 minutes. Season to taste with salt and pepper.
4. Serve the spinach balls in the soup.

*4 to 6 servings*

# Tortilla-Ball Soup

8 large stale tortillas
1 cup milk
1 small onion, coarsely chopped
1 clove garlic, minced
¼ cup grated Parmesan cheese
1 whole egg plus 1 egg yolk,
    beaten
½ teaspoon salt
⅛ teaspoon pepper
    Lard or oil for frying
2 quarts meat stock (see recipe on
    page 56), or 2 quarts canned
    beef broth (3 cans condensed
    beef broth plus equal amount
    water)
1 cup canned tomato sauce

1. Tear tortillas into pieces and soak in milk until soft. Place in an electric blender with onion and garlic and blend until puréed. Turn purée into a bowl. Beat in cheese, whole egg and egg yolk, salt, and pepper. Shape into small balls.
2. Fry in hot lard until lightly browned.
3. Meanwhile, heat meat stock and tomato sauce together in a large kettle. When bubbling, add tortilla balls. Serve at once.

*6 to 8 servings*

# Mexican Rice

2 cups uncooked rice
¼ cup oil
1 cup coarsely chopped onion (1
    medium onion)
1 clove garlic, minced
1 cup canned tomato sauce
1 quart beef or chicken stock (or 1
    quart water plus 4 bouillon
    cubes)
2 teaspoons chili powder
1 cup peas (fresh, frozen, or
    canned—cooked or uncooked)

1. Cook rice in hot oil in a skillet about 10 minutes, stirring frequently.
2. Meanwhile, combine onion, garlic, and tomato sauce in an electric blender and blend until liquefied.
3. Stir onion-tomato mixture into rice and cook about 10 minutes.
4. Add stock, chili powder, and uncooked peas (if using); stir until well mixed. Bring to boiling, cover tightly, reduce heat to simmering, and cook about 20 minutes, or until all water is absorbed by rice.
5. If using cooked peas, mix with the rice. Heat thoroughly.

*8 to 10 servings*

# Green Rice

1 cup (1 small can) salsa verde
    mexicana (Mexican green
    tomato sauce)
1 cup (lightly packed) fresh parsley
1 clove garlic
2 tablespoons vegetable oil
2 cups beef or chicken stock, or 2
    cups water plus 2 bouillon
    cubes
    Salt and pepper
1 cup uncooked rice

1. Put salsa verde, parsley, and garlic in an electric blender and blend until liquefied.
2. Heat oil in a large saucepan. Add blended sauce and mix well; cook about 5 minutes.
3. Add stock to saucepan and bring to boiling, stirring to blend ingredients. Season to taste with salt and pepper. Add rice, stir, cover tightly, and cook until all liquid is absorbed (about 25 minutes).

*6 servings*

# Baked Green Rice

3 cups hot cooked rice
2 cups shredded Monterey Jack or
    mild Cheddar cheese
⅓ cup butter
1 can (4 ounces) green chilies,
    drained, seeded, and chopped
1 cup finely chopped parsley
1 small onion, chopped
1 teaspoon salt
¼ teaspoon pepper
2 eggs, beaten
1 cup milk

1. Combine hot rice with cheese and butter. Toss until well mixed. Add chilies, parsley, onion, salt, and pepper; mix. Add beaten eggs and milk; mix until blended.
2. Turn into a greased 2-quart baking dish. Cover dish.
3. Bake at 350°F 30 minutes. Uncover; bake 10 minutes.

*About 8 servings*

# Cumin Rice

2 tablespoons butter
2 cups coarsely chopped red or
    green sweet peppers
⅓ cup chopped onion
1 clove garlic, finely chopped
1 teaspoon cumin (comino)
1½ cups uncooked rice
1½ cups hot chicken broth

1. Heat butter in a saucepan. Add peppers and onion and cook until onion is soft. Add garlic, cumin, rice, and hot broth; mix well. Cover saucepan.
2. Bring to boiling, reduce heat, and cook about 20 minutes, or until rice is tender and liquid is absorbed.

*About 8 servings*

# Macaroni Mexicana

8 ounces macaroni
2 fresh or dried ancho chilies
1 cup whipping cream
½ teaspoon salt
1 cup shredded Monterey Jack or
    mild Cheddar cheese
    Paprika

1. Cook macaroni until just tender, following package directions. Drain.
2. Meanwhile, wash, peel, and seed chilies (see page 30). Chop prepared chilies and put into an electric blender. Add cream and salt. Blend until chilies are finely chopped.
3. Layer in a greased 1½-quart casserole: cooked macaroni, cheese, then sauce. Sprinkle top with paprika.
4. Bake at 350°F about 30 minutes, or until bubbling hot.

*6 servings*

# Dry Soup of Tortillas with Tomatoes and Cheese

½ cup oil
1 cup chopped onion
1 clove garlic, minced
2 cups (16-ounce can) cooked tomatoes with juice, slightly chopped
1 teaspoon salt
¼ teaspoon pepper
½ teaspoon oregano
10 to 12 stale tortillas, cut in ½-inch strips
1 cup whipping cream
1 cup (about ¼ pound) grated Parmesan cheese
Paprika

1. Heat 2 tablespoons oil in a heavy saucepan. Cook onion and garlic in hot oil until onion is soft (about 5 minutes). Add tomatoes, salt, pepper, and oregano and stir until blended. Heat to simmering and cook about 10 minutes to blend flavors.
2. Meanwhile, heat remaining oil in a heavy skillet. Fry tortilla strips in hot oil until limp, not crisp; drain on paper towels.
3. In an ovenproof casserole arrange layers as follows: a little tomato sauce, a handful of tortilla strips, some cream, then cheese. Repeat until all ingredients are used, ending with cheese. Sprinkle with paprika.
4. Bake at 350°F about 20 minutes, or until bubbling hot.

*6 servings*

# Baked Noodles with Chorizo

¼ pound chorizo sausage (see Chorizo Filling, page 18) or use bulk pork sausage
2 to 4 tablespoons lard or oil
1 package (7 ounces) fine noodles
¼ cup chopped onion
2 cups beef or chicken stock, or water plus bouillon cubes
1 cup cottage cheese
1 cup dairy sour cream
Dash Tabasco (if bulk pork sausage used)
Salt and pepper
Grated Parmesan cheese

1. Fry chorizo in a large skillet with heat-resistant handle until cooked through, crumbling and stirring as it cooks.
2. Remove meat from skillet and set aside. Add lard or oil to skillet to make about 1¼-inch layer in bottom. Stir in uncooked noodles and onion and fry until noodles are lightly browned and onion is soft, stirring often to prevent burning.
3. Return cooked chorizo to skillet. Stir in stock.
4. Bake at 350°F about 15 minutes, or until all liquid is absorbed by noodles.
5. Remove skillet from oven. Stir in cottage cheese and sour cream. Season to taste with Tabasco, if using, and salt and pepper to taste. Sprinkle with Parmesan cheese. Return to oven and bake about 10 minutes, or until bubbling hot.

*6 servings*

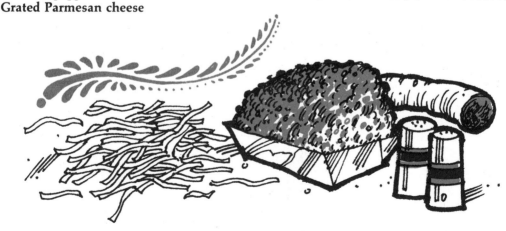

At Christmas each year Mexicans traditionally serve **Christmas Eve Salad, 66.**

## SALADS

Salads served as a side dish with the entrée are not really among traditional Mexican foods, even though salad ingredients are plentiful in Mexican markets. Usually these foods—lettuce, radishes, raw cabbage and onions, and tomatoes, for example—are used as garnishes for tacos, enchiladas, and other similar dishes. What we in the United States think of as a salad may be served as the first course of a big meal. Or it may become a condiment for its flavor and texture contrast. Included in this section are several traditional saladlike dishes, plus recipes for favorite Mexican foods used in somewhat untraditional salads. The more filling of these will make excellent luncheon main dishes, while the lighter ones can assume our typical salad role.

Avocados are so readily available in Mexican markets that they are used frequently. They most often appear in the universally popular guacamole, which Mexicans eat as a condiment and North Americans often serve as a dip. Another delicious way to eat this creamy fruit is with a zesty salad filling, ideal for an appetizer or even an entrée for luncheon.

# Guacamole I

2 **very ripe avocados**
1 **medium fresh tomato**
1 **small onion, chopped (about ⅓ cup)**
2 **tablespoons lemon juice**
1 **teaspoon salt**
1 **to 2 teaspoons chili powder**

1. Peel avocados and mash pulp, leaving a few small lumps throughout.
2. Peel and chop tomato and add to mashed avocado. Add onion, lemon juice, salt, and chili powder to taste. If not serving immediately, refrigerate in covered bowl, with avocado pits immersed in guacamole; this is said to help keep avocado from darkening on standing.
3. Serve on lettuce as a salad, as a "dip" with tostada chips, or as a condiment to top taco fillings.

*About 2 cups guacamole*

*Note:* If you prefer a smoother guacamole, ingredients may be blended to desired consistency.

# Guacamole II

2 **large ripe avocados**
3 **tablespoons lemon juice**
1 **medium tomato**
1 **slice onion**
1 **small green chili**
1 **small clove garlic, minced**
⅛ **teaspoon coriander**
**Salt**

1. Halve avocados, peel, remove pits, and cut avocado into pieces. Put into an electric blender with lemon juice.
2. Peel, halve, and seed tomato. Add to blender along with onion, chili, garlic, coriander, and salt to taste. Blend.
3. Serve as a dip with **corn chips, cauliflowerets,** and **carrot** and **celery sticks.**

*About 3 cups dip*

The "brave bull" piñata has an eye on a serving of **Avocados Stuffed with Cauliflower Salad, 67.**

# Christmas Eve Salad *(Ensalada de Noche Buena)*

*This salad is customarily served at the traditional Mexican midnight supper on Christmas Eve. It usually precedes a turkey entrée. You might enjoy it in a similar menu. Or, it could provide an interestingly different light luncheon main dish.*

1 cup diced cooked beets
1 cup diced tart apple, not peeled
1 cup orange sections
1 cup sliced bananas
1 cup diced pineapple (fresh or canned)
   Juice of 1 lime
   Oil and Vinegar Dressing (see below)
   Shredded lettuce
½ cup chopped peanuts
   Seeds from 1 pomegranate

1. Drain beets well. Combine beets, apple, oranges, bananas, and pineapple. Refrigerate until ready to serve.
2. Add lime juice to beet-fruit mixture. Add desired amount of dressing and toss until evenly mixed and coated with dressing.
3. To serve, make a bed of shredded lettuce in salad bowl. Mound salad on top. Sprinkle with peanuts and pomegranate seeds.

*8 to 10 servings*

*Oil and Vinegar Dressing:* Mix **2 tablespoons white wine vinegar, 1½ teaspoons sugar, and ¼ teaspoon salt.** Add **⅓ cup salad oil;** mix well.

Pico de Gallo is a perfect accompaniment for spicy Mexican dishes like enchiladas and tamales, and is often served just that way. But it is also frequently prepared fresh by street vendors as a finger food for stand-up diners. And thereby this crunchy salad received its name. For the actions of eating with the fingers is compared to the motions of a rooster pecking at corn in the farm yard. Pico de Gallo calls for the Mexican root vegetable jícama, which has a flavor and crisp texture similar to water chestnuts. If jícama is unavailable through local Mexican markets, tart, crisp apples may be substituted. This will produce a delicious salad even though the flavor will not be authentic.

# Rooster's Bill *(Pico de Gallo)*

1 medium jícama*
1 large orange
¼ cup chopped onion
   Juice of 1 lemon
1 teaspoon salt
1 teaspoon chili powder
½ teaspoon oregano, crumbled

*3 large tart crisp apples may be substituted for jícama.

1. Wash, pare, and chop jícama into ½-inch chunks.
2. Pare and section orange, reserving juice, and add to jícama; pour orange juice over fruit chunks. Add onion, lemon juice, and salt and stir until evenly mixed. Let stand at least 1 hour in refrigerator before serving.
3. When ready to serve, sprinkle with chili powder and oregano.

*4 to 6 servings*

# Avocados Stuffed with Cauliflower Salad

2 cups very small, crisp raw
   cauliflowerets
1 cup cooked green peas
½ cup sliced ripe olives
¼ cup chopped pimento
¼ cup chopped onion
   Oil and Vinegar Dressing (see
      page 66)
   Salt to taste
6 small lettuce leaves
3 large ripe avocados
   Lemon wedges

1. Combine all ingredients, except lettuce, avocados, and lemon wedges; stir gently until evenly mixed and coated with dressing.
2. Refrigerate at least 1 hour before serving.
3. When ready to serve, peel, halve, and remove pits from avocados. Place a lettuce leaf on each serving plate; top with avocado half filled with a mound of cauliflower salad. Serve with lemon wedges.

*6 servings*

# Coliflor Acapulco

1 large head cauliflower
   Marinade (see below)
1 can (15 ounces) garbanzos,
   drained
1 cup pimento-stuffed olives
   Pimentos, drained and cut
      lengthwise in strips
   Lettuce
1 jar (16 ounces) sliced pickled
   beets, drained and chilled
1 large cucumber, thinly sliced and
   chilled
   Parsley sprigs
   Radish roses
   Guacamole I (page 65)

1. Bring 1 inch of salted water to boiling in a large saucepan. Add cauliflower, cover, and cook about 20 minutes, or until just tender; drain.
2. Place cauliflower, head down, in a deep bowl and pour marinade over it. Chill several hours or overnight; occasionally spoon marinade over all.
3. Shortly before serving, thread garbanzos, olives, and pimento strips onto wooden picks for decorative kabobs. Set aside while arranging salad.
4. Drain cauliflower. Line a chilled serving plate with lettuce and place cauliflower, head up, in the center. Arrange pickled beet and cucumber slices around the base, tucking in parsley sprigs and radish roses.
5. Spoon and spread guacamole over cauliflower. Decorate with kabobs. Serve cold.

*6 to 8 servings*

*Marinade:* Combine **1½ cups vegetable oil, ½ cup lemon juice, 1½ teaspoons salt,** and **1 teaspoon chili powder.** Shake marinade well before using.

# Carrot Salad

6 large fresh carrots, very thinly
   sliced or grated
½ cup raisins
¾ cup orange juice
1 teaspoon sugar
⅛ teaspoon salt

Combine all ingredients and refrigerate at least 30 minutes before serving.

*4 servings*

# Garbanzo Salad

1 **can (15 ounces) garbanzos,
    drained**
¼ **cup chopped parsley**
1 **can or jar (4 ounces) pimentos,
    drained and chopped**
3 **green onions, chopped**
¼ **cup wine vinegar**
2 **tablespoons olive or salad oil**
1 **teaspoon salt**
½ **teaspoon sugar**
¼ **teaspoon pepper**

Combine all ingredients in a bowl; cover and refrigerate until chilled.

*About 6 servings*

# Shrimp Salad

1½ **cups cooked shrimp, sliced in
    half lengthwise**
½ **cup diced cooked potatoes**
2 **hard-cooked eggs, sliced**
½ **cup chopped celery**
¼ **cup chopped green onions**
½ **cup mayonnaise or salad
    dressing**
½ **cup dairy sour cream**
½ **teaspoon chili powder**
  **Salt to taste**
  **Lettuce leaves**
  **Lemon wedges**

1. Combine all ingredients, except lettuce and lemon wedges, and stir gently until evenly mixed and coated with dressing.
2. Refrigerate at least 1 hour before serving.
3. When ready to serve, place on lettuce leaves. Serve with lemon wedges.

*6 servings*

*Note:* Shrimp salad also makes a delicious avocado filling.

# Cucumber Mousse

1 **package (3 ounces) lime-flavored
    gelatin**
¾ **cup boiling water**
1 **cup cottage cheese**
1 **cup mayonnaise or salad dressing**
2 **tablespoons grated onion**
¾ **cup grated cucumber**
1 **cup slivered almonds**

1. Dissolve gelatin in boiling water. Stir in cottage cheese, mayonnaise, and onion until well blended. Fold in cucumber and almonds.
2. Pour mixture into a 1-quart mold. Refrigerate until set.

*4 to 6 servings*

## VEGETABLES

Mexican cooks have a wide variety of vegetables from which to choose. And as you might expect, they usually prepare them in spicy sauces, much like those used with other dishes in the menu. Some favorite vegetables are greens (familiar kinds like spinach and kale, plus others not available in the United States), several types of squash, peas, sweet corn, green beans, cauliflower, cabbage, and carrots. Here is a sampling of typical recipes for vegetables Mexican-style. Use your imagination with your favorites, using these ideas as guidelines.

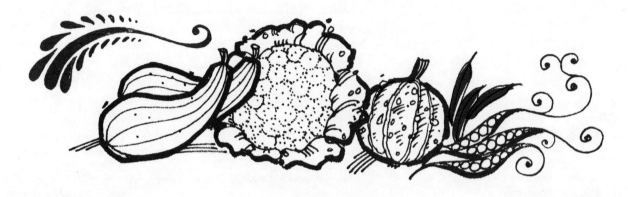

# Garbanzos with Condiments

¼ pound bulk pork sausage
½ cup chopped onion
1 clove garlic, minced
1 teaspoon chili powder
2 cups (16-ounce can) cooked garbanzos, drained and rinsed
1 can (4 ounces) pimentos, drained and cut in strips
Salt
¼ teaspoon oregano
⅛ teaspoon pepper

1. Brown sausage in skillet, crumbling and stirring as it cooks. Add onion, garlic, and chili powder and cook until onion is soft. Add garbanzos and pimentos and stir to mix well. Bring to simmering. Season to taste with salt; add oregano and pepper.
2. Serve as an accompaniment to meat.

*4 to 6 servings*

# Cauliflower Tortas

1 head cauliflower
2 eggs, separated
2 tablespoons flour
1 teaspoon salt
Dash pepper
Oil or shortening for deep frying heated to 375°F

1. Rinse cauliflower, remove outer leaves, and separate into cauliflowerets. Cook in boiling salted water until almost tender (about 8 to 10 minutes). Drain.
2. Beat egg whites until they form rounded peaks. Beat egg yolks until smooth. Pour yolks into whites gradually, beating lightly with fork to combine.
3. In separate small bowl combine flour, salt, and pepper. Roll cooked cauliflowerets, a few at a time, in flour, then dip in eggs, coating well.
4. Fry in heated fat until golden brown, turning to brown on all sides. Serve very hot.

*8 to 10 servings*

# Lima Beans Mexicana

2 packages (10 ounces each) frozen
    green lima beans
2 tablespoons butter or margarine
½ cup chopped onion
1 clove garlic, minced
1 cup canned tomatoes
1 jalapeño chili, chopped
    Salt and pepper
1 hard-cooked egg, chopped

1. Cook beans until tender, following package directions.
2. Meanwhile, heat butter in a small skillet. Add onion and garlic and cook about 5 minutes, until onion is soft. Stir in tomatoes and chili. Season to taste with salt and pepper.
3. Drain beans. Pour tomato sauce over beans and stir gently until evenly mixed. Turn into a serving dish and garnish with chopped hard-cooked egg.

*6 servings*

# Corn-Chili Casserole

1 can (17 ounces) cream style corn
1 can (4 ounces) chopped green
    chilies (undrained)
2 eggs, beaten
2 tablespoons flour
1 teaspoon sugar
½ teaspoon salt
⅛ teaspoon oregano
1 tablespoon butter

1. Mix corn, chilies, and eggs. Blend flour, sugar, salt, and oregano; stir into corn mixture. Turn into a greased 1-quart casserole. Dot with butter.
2. Bake at 350°F 55 to 60 minutes, or until set.

*About 6 servings*

# Chili-Hominy Casserole

2 cans (15 ounces each) whole
    hominy, drained and rinsed
1 can (4 ounces) green chilies,
    drained (discard seeds) and
    finely chopped
1 tablespoon butter
1½ cups dairy sour cream
    Salt and pepper
1 cup shredded Monterey Jack or
    mild Cheddar cheese

1. Layer half of hominy and the chopped chilies in a well-buttered 1½-quart baking dish. Dot with butter and spread with half of sour cream. Add a layer of remaining hominy, cover with remaining sour cream, and sprinkle with salt and pepper to taste. Top with cheese.
2. Bake at 350°F about 25 minutes, or just until thoroughly heated.

*About 6 servings*

# Hominy and Bacon

½ pound sliced bacon
1 green pepper, chopped
1 small onion, chopped
1 can (16 ounces) tomatoes
    (undrained)
1 tablespoon sugar
1 teaspoon salt
2 cans (15 ounces each) whole
    hominy, drained

1. Fry bacon in a skillet until lightly browned; drain. Reserve 2 tablespoons drippings in skillet. Mix in green pepper and onion; cook until tender. Add tomatoes with liquid, sugar, and salt; simmer 10 minutes.
2. Turn hominy into a greased shallow baking dish; crumble bacon over top and mix with hominy. Pour tomato mixture over all.
3. Bake at 325°F about 45 minutes.

*6 to 8 servings*

# Hominy in Tomato Sauce

1 can (15 ounces) whole hominy, drained
1 can (16 ounces) tomatoes
1 tablespoon chili powder
½ teaspoon salt
1 medium onion, chopped
8 ounces sharp Cheddar cheese, shredded

1. Combine hominy and tomatoes in a saucepan. Cook, stirring occasionally, until thickened (about 15 minutes). Stir in chili powder, salt, and onion.
2. Layer hominy and cheese in a shallow 1½-quart baking dish, ending with cheese.
3. Bake at 350°F about 20 minutes.

*About 6 servings*

# Green Chili Cornbread I

1 cup yellow cornmeal
2 teaspoons baking powder
½ teaspoon salt
2 eggs
¼ cup vegetable oil
1 can (4 ounces) green chilies, drained, seeded, and finely chopped
1 can (8 ounces) cream style corn
½ cup dairy sour cream
2 cups shredded mild Cheddar cheese

1. Mix cornmeal, baking powder, and salt; set aside.
2. Beat eggs with oil until blended. Add chilies, corn, sour cream, cornmeal mixture, and 1½ cups cheese; mix well.
3. Turn into a greased 9-inch round pan. Sprinkle with remaining cheese.
4. Bake at 350°F 45 minutes, or until lightly browned.
5. Serve warm with butter, if desired.

*6 to 8 servings*

# Green Chili Cornbread II

1½ cups cornmeal
1½ tablespoons flour
1 tablespoon salt
½ teaspoon baking soda
1 cup buttermilk
⅔ cup vegetable oil
2 eggs, beaten
1 can (8 ounces) cream style corn
1 can (about 4 ounces) chopped green chilies, drained
4 green onions, chopped
1½ cups shredded Monterey Jack

1. Mix cornmeal, flour, salt, and baking soda in a bowl. Add buttermilk, oil, eggs, and corn; mix well. Stir in chilies and onions.
2. Grease a 13×9-inch baking dish with **bacon fat;** heat in oven.
3. Pour half of batter into heated pan and sprinkle with half of cheese; repeat, using remaining batter and cheese.
4. Bake at 375°F about 35 minutes.
5. Cut into squares and serve warm.

*8 to 12 servings*

# Cornbread Pie

1 cup soft butter or margarine
1 cup sugar
4 eggs
2 cups (17-ounce can) cream style
    corn
1 cup shredded Monterey Jack
1 can (4 ounces) green chilies,
    drained, seeded, and chopped
1 cup yellow or white cornmeal
1 cup sifted all-purpose flour
4 teaspoons baking powder
½ teaspoon salt

1. Cream butter and sugar until light and fluffy. Beat in eggs, one at a time. Stir in corn, cheese, chilies, and cornmeal.
2. Sift flour, baking powder, and salt together and stir into batter.
3. Pour into greased 13×9-inch baking pan or two 9-inch pie pans.
4. Bake at 300°F 60 to 70 minutes, or until a wooden pick inserted in center comes out clean.
5. To serve, cut while still hot into squares or wedges. Serve with butter, if desired.

*6 to 8 servings*

# Mexican Eggplant

1 eggplant (¾ to 1 pound)
2 cloves garlic
1 large green pepper
1 can (4 ounces) hot green chilies,
    drained and seeded
2 tablespoons olive oil
1 can (6 ounces) tomato paste
⅔ cup water
1 teaspoon salt
⅛ teaspoon pepper
2 eggs
¼ cup olive oil
1 cup shredded Monterey Jack or
    mild Cheddar cheese

1. Pare eggplant and cut into ¼-inch slices; set aside.
2. Finely chop garlic, pepper, and chilies. Sauté in olive oil until soft. Add tomato paste, water, and salt and pepper to taste. Simmer, stirring occasionally, until sauce is thickened.
3. Beat eggs and coat eggplant slices with egg.
4. Heat olive oil in a large skillet, add eggplant, and quickly brown on both sides.
5. Put browned eggplant into a shallow baking dish, cover with sauce, and sprinkle with cheese.
6. Bake at 350°F about 30 minutes, or until eggplant is tender and cheese is lightly browned.

*About 6 servings*

# Greens with Chilies

3 fresh or dried ancho chilies
1½ pounds fresh greens (spinach,
    kale, collard greens, mustard
    greens, Swiss chard, etc.)
2 tablespoons butter or margarine
½ cup chopped onion
1 clove garlic, minced
    Salt and pepper

1. Prepare chilies (see page 30) and chop them.
2. Wash greens well. Cook in small amount of boiling salted water until tender. Drain and chop. Return to saucepan.
3. Melt butter in a small skillet. Add chilies, onion, and garlic and cook until onion is soft, about 5 minutes. Stir chili mixture into chopped greens. Season to taste with salt and pepper. Heat thoroughly.

*6 servings*

# Peas with Condiments

2 packages (10 ounces each) frozen
   green peas
2 tablespoons butter or margarine
½ cup chopped onion
3 canned pimentos, cut in 1-inch
   strips
   Salt and pepper

1. Cook peas until tender, following package directions.
2. Meanwhile, heat butter in a small skillet. Add onion and cook about 5 minutes, or until onion is soft. Stir in pimento.
3. Drain peas. Stir onion and pimento into peas. Season to taste with salt and pepper.

*6 servings*

# Aztec Patties

*This unique use for leftover mashed potatoes is a well-known Mexican side dish. If you live in an area where fresh masa is available, use that in place of the dehydrated masa flour and water.*

1 cup dehydrated masa flour
   (masa harina)
¾ cup warm water
1½ cups mashed potatoes
   Salt (about 1 teaspoon)
½ cup shredded Monterey Jack
1 egg, beaten
   Lard or oil

1. Mix masa flour with warm water until dough can be formed into a soft ball. Combine with mashed potatoes and mix well. Stir in salt to taste, then add cheese and beaten egg. Form into patties about ¾ inch thick.
2. Fry patties in hot lard in a skillet.
3. Serve as an accompaniment to meat.

*6 to 8 servings*

# Squash and Corn Dish

2 tablespoons oil
⅓ cup chopped onion
1 small clove garlic, minced
2 pounds summer squash, pared
   and cubed
1 cup whole kernel corn, drained
1 large fresh tomato, peeled and
   cubed
1 jalapeño chili, finely chopped
1 teaspoon salt
¼ teaspoon pepper
½ cup milk
   Grated Parmesan cheese

1. Heat oil in a skillet that can be transferred to oven. Add onion and garlic and cook until soft (about 5 minutes). Add squash, corn, tomato, chili, salt, and pepper and cook over low heat about 10 minutes, stirring occasionally. If skillet cannot be put into oven, transfer mixture to an ovenproof dish; pour milk over top.
2. Bake at 350°F about 30 minutes.
3. Remove from oven and sprinkle with Parmesan cheese.

*About 8 servings*

# Spinach with Tomato

2 packages (10 ounces each) fresh
   spinach
3 slices bacon
2 tablespoons bacon fat
½ cup chopped onion
1 cup chopped fresh tomato
¾ teaspoon salt
⅛ teaspoon pepper

1. Wash spinach thoroughly. Put spinach with water that clings to leaves into a large saucepan. Cook rapidly about 5 minutes, or until tender. Drain.
2. Meanwhile, fry bacon until crisp in a large skillet. Drain bacon, crumble, and set aside. Add onion to 2 tablespoons bacon fat in skillet and cook until soft. Add tomato, spinach, salt, and pepper. Heat thoroughly.
3. Garnish with sliced hard-cooked egg, if desired.

*About 6 servings*

# Green Tomatoes and Zucchini

2 tablespoons butter
1 large onion, chopped
¾ cup chopped canned Mexican
    green tomatoes (tomatillos)
3 medium zucchini, thinly sliced
½ teaspoon oregano
½ teaspoon salt
1 tablespoon water
¼ cup grated Parmesan cheese

1. Heat butter in a large skillet. Add onion and cook until soft. Add green tomatoes, zucchini, oregano, salt, and water; stir. Cover; bring to boiling, reduce heat, and cook until zucchini is crisp-tender (5 to 7 minutes).
2. Stir in cheese just before serving.

*6 to 8 servings*

# Baked Zucchini

2 pounds zucchini
1 cup shredded mild Cheddar
    cheese
½ cup cottage cheese
4 eggs, beaten
¾ cup dry bread crumbs
3 tablespoons chopped parsley
1½ teaspoons salt
½ teaspoon pepper
3 tablespoons butter

1. Wash zucchini and slice crosswise into ¼-inch slices. (It is not necessary to peel zucchini, unless skin seems very tough.)
2. Combine cheeses, eggs, bread crumbs, parsley, salt, and pepper until evenly mixed. Layer into baking dish, alternating zucchini with sauce. Dot top with butter.
3. Bake at 375°F about 45 minutes, or until slightly set.

*6 to 8 servings*

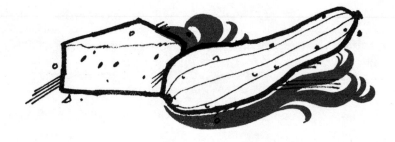

# BEVERAGES

Mexicans drink many of the same beverages as North Americans. Notably, they consume lots of coffee, the importance of which is demonstrated by the large number of special coffee stores in which the customer may have the grind blended to his own taste. Then too, beverages made with chocolate are popular. After all, Mexico is the home of chocolate. When the Spaniards conquered Mexico they liberated chocolate for the rest of the world. Up until that time it had been reserved for royalty and the high priests. Now, a chocolate-flavored bottled soft drink is made.

Of course, many varieties of fruit juices are consumed, both fresh and canned, as well as vast quantities of familiar bottled soft drinks. And Mexican beer is delicious, with an excellent reputation away from home. Tea is probably the one major beverage not consumed in great quatities.

Included here are a selection of beverage recipes which are typically Mexican, some of which have become well known outside their native land, and some which haven't yet been exported.

## Coffee with Milk (*Café con Leche*)

**Hot coffee**
**Hot milk**

Make coffee by your usual method, using about 2 times your usual amount of coffee. Serve it with a pitcher of hot milk, so each person can dilute his brew to his own taste.

## Mexican Coffee

1 quart water
⅔ cup firmly packed brown sugar
⅔ cup ground coffee

1. Heat water and brown sugar in a saucepan. When sugar is dissolved, add coffee. Let boil 2 minutes.
2. Remove from heat and stir well. Cover and keep hot until all the coffee is at the bottom; strain and serve.

*About 12 servings*

# Mexican Hot Chocolate

**Mexican chocolate**
**Warm milk**

1. For authentic Mexican flavor, purchase cakes of Mexican chocolate in a specialty grocery store. These are presweetened chocolate, flavored with cinnamon and, sometimes, ground almonds. The cakes are generally marked off to indicate how much to use with 1 cup of warm milk for a single serving of hot chocolate. (On the other hand, American cocoa can be used, too. Just follow package directions for the amounts of sugar and milk and cooking method. Then add a bit of cinnamon and a drop or two of almond extract.)
2. Beat well with an egg beater to achieve a foamy top. (Mexicans use a wooden gadget which looks somewhat like a darning ball with a long handle, with loose wooden rings around the ball section. This "molinello" is operated by placing the ball end in the chocolate and spinning the handle back and forth between the palms of the hands.)

Atole is an unusual but historic drink, which uses corn masa, the same ingredient basic to both tortillas and tamales. It is often served with tamales, and may be served plain or flavored with nuts or fruits. When flavored with chocolate it is always called Champurrado, even though it is still the same basic drink. Atoles are highly nourishing, and simple enough to make that they're worth trying just for fun.

# Basic Atole

½ cup dehydrated masa flour
   (masa harina)
3 cups water
1 cinnamon stick
1 cup sugar
1½ cups crushed fruit, such as
   strawberries or pineapple
   (optional)
3 cups milk

1. Put masa flour into a saucepan and stir in water. Add cinnamon stick. Cook over low heat, stirring constantly, until slightly thickened. Add sugar, fruit if desired, and milk. Continue to heat, stirring to dissolve sugar, to just below boiling.
2. Ladle into mugs.

Almond Atole: Substitute ½ **cup ground blanched almonds** for the fruit. After atole is reheated to just below boiling, remove from heat and stir in **3 beaten egg yolks.**

Champurrado: Substitute **brown sugar** for the white sugar and add **3 ounces (3 squares) unsweetened chocolate,** grated, instead of the fruit. Beat with a rotary beater until frothy.

# Rompope

*Rompope is a Mexican-style eggnog, which you might enjoy for holiday parties as a variation of the traditional American type. This may be bottled and stored quite a long time in the refrigerator.*

1 quart milk
1 cup sugar
1 stick cinnamon
¼ cup finely ground almonds
1 teaspoon vanilla extract
8 egg yolks
1 cup light rum, brandy, or grain alcohol

1. Put milk, sugar, and cinnamon stick into a saucepan. Heat to simmering, and simmer gently, stirring constantly, about 10 minutes.
2. Remove from heat and remove cinnamon stick. Add almonds and vanilla extract.
3. Beat egg yolks until thick and lemon-colored. Gradually beat into milk. Return to heat and cook over low heat, stirring constantly, until mixture coats a spoon. Cool to room temperature.
4. Mix in rum and pour into a large bottle with screw lid. Refrigerate until ready to serve.

*About 1½ quarts*

# Sangría

*Sangría originated in Spain, but is so popular in Mexico that there is now a bottled, carbonated soft drink version. This recipe is for the alcoholic type, really a fruit-flavored wine. To turn sangría into a refreshing punch, just add a bottle of sparkling water.*

⅓ cup lime juice
½ cup orange juice
½ cup sugar
1 bottle (⅘ quart) dry red wine
   Ice cubes

1. Combine lime and orange juices with sugar; stir until sugar is dissolved. Stir into wine in a pitcher. Chill before serving.
2. To serve, pour over ice cubes in tall glasses.

*About 1 quart*

# Tía María

*This might be called ".do-it-yourself-Kaluha," though it doesn't really replace that delicious liqueur.*

2 cups water
4 cups sugar
5 tablespoons instant coffee
1 tablespoon vanilla extract
1 bottle (⅘ quart) vodka or grain alcohol

1. Combine water and sugar in saucepan. Bring to boiling, reduce heat, and simmer about 20 minutes.
2. Remove from heat; stir in coffee and vanilla extract, then vodka.
3. Pour into a bottle with a screw lid and store 1 month before using.

*About 5 cups*

In Mexico there are a number of different alcoholic beverages made from various varieties of the maguey plant (also called the agave or century plant). The most famous of these is tequila, the production of which is big business in Mexico. Two others, mezcal, a distilled drink similar to tequila but made only regionally, and pulque, which is prepared from the fermented sap of the maguey, are little known outside of Mexico. They are seldom more than tasted by visitors. However, pulque is of interest in Mexican cooking because it is an essential ingredient in the famous Salsa Borracha (drunken sauce) traditionally served with elaborate "pibil" recipes (whole animals barbecued in a pit).

Every visitor to Mexico has certainly tried the most famous tequila cocktail, the Margarita. Two other sweeter tequila-based cocktails also follow.

# Margarita

Juice of ½ lime
Coarse salt, if available, or
   regular table salt
2 ounces tequila
½ ounce Cointreau
Crushed ice

1. Wet rim of a cocktail glass with the lime rind. Spin the glass in a saucer of salt to coat rim.
2. Combine tequila, Cointreau, and lime juice in a cocktail shaker; add ice. Shake or stir until well chilled.
3. Strain into salt-rimmed glass.

*1 serving*

# Tequila Sour

1 teaspoon sugar
3 ounces tequila
Juice of ½ lemon
Dash Angostura bitters
Crushed ice
Sparkling water

1. Dissolve sugar in tequila in a cocktail shaker. Add lemon juice, bitters, and ice. Shake or stir until well chilled.
2. Strain into an old-fashioned glass. Add a splash of sparkling water.

*1 serving*

# Tequila Cocktail

1½ ounces tequila
Juice of 1 lime
½ ounce grenadine
Crushed ice

1. Combine in a cocktail shaker and shake or stir until well chilled.
2. Strain into a cocktail glass.

*1 serving*

# DESSERTS AND SWEET BREADS

The dessert most frequently offered on the Mexican restaurant menu is Flan. Inherited from Spain as plain baked custard with a baked-in caramel layer, this dessert when prepared at home may well sport an added ingredient such as coconut, almonds, pineapple, or bananas. Many other pudding-type desserts made with tropical fruits, nuts, wine, and spices are popular, as well. For the North American taste, you might prefer to serve a fresh fruit platter as the complementary finale to spicy Mexican foods.

There are a number of fancy sweet yeast breads which are traditionally baked for special religious days. Often these also contain fruits and/or nuts. Cinnamon is the most popularly used spice, and may appear in desserts, breads, cookies, and snacks.

## Coconut Flan

*Flan is a baked custard dessert which Mexico has adopted from Spain. A caramelized layer is prepared in the bottom of the baking dish before the custard is poured in, so when the finished dessert is turned out it has a caramel topping. This version is flavored with coconut.*

**Caramel Topping:**
- ½ cup granulated sugar
- 2 tablespoons water

**Custard:**
- 2 cups milk
- 4 eggs
- ¼ cup sugar
- ⅛ teaspoon salt
- ½ teaspoon vanilla extract
- ⅓ cup shredded or flaked coconut

1. For caramel topping, heat sugar and water in a small skillet, stirring constantly, until sugar melts and turns golden brown.

2. Pour syrup into a 1-quart baking dish or 6 custard cups, tipping to coat bottom and part way up sides. Set dish aside while preparing custard.

3. For custard, scald milk. Beat eggs; beat in sugar, salt, and vanilla extract. Gradually beat scalded milk into egg mixture. Strain into prepared baking dish or custard cups. Sprinkle top with coconut.

4. Place baking dish in pan containing hot water which comes at least 1 inch up sides of dish.

5. Bake at 325°F about 45 minutes for individual custard cups, or 1 hour for baking dish.

*6 servings*

# Quick Flan

*This is a somewhat simpler recipe for flan, made with sweetened condensed milk and "baked" in a pressure cooker. The flavor's a bit different, too.*

¼ cup granulated sugar
4 eggs
1 can (14 ounces) sweetened
   condensed milk
½ can water
1 teaspoon vanilla extract

1. Select a pan of at least 1-quart capacity which will fit inside pressure cooker. Spread sugar over bottom of pan. Heat over very low heat, stirring constantly, until sugar melts and turns golden brown. Remove from heat.
2. Beat eggs in a bowl; beat in milk, water, and vanilla extract.
3. Pour milk-egg mixture into sugar-coated pan.
4. Place about 1 inch of water in pressure cooker. Place filled pan inside cooker. Lay a sheet of waxed paper over top of milk-egg mixture. Place cover on cooker and heat following manufacturer's directions; cook 10 minutes.
5. Cool, then chill before serving.

*6 servings*

# Bread Pudding (Capirotada)

2 cups firmly packed dark brown
   sugar
1 quart water
1 stick cinnamon
1 clove
6 slices toast, cubed
3 apples, pared, cored, and sliced
1 cup raisins
1 cup chopped blanched almonds
½ pound Monterey Jack or similar
   cheese, cubed

1. Put brown sugar, water, cinnamon, and clove into a saucepan and bring to boiling; reduce heat and simmer until a light syrup is formed. Discard spices and set syrup aside.
2. Meanwhile, arrange a layer of toast cubes in a buttered casserole. Cover with a layer of apples, raisins, almonds, and cheese. Repeat until all ingredients are used. Pour syrup over all.
3. Bake at 350°F about 30 minutes.
4. Serve hot.

*6 servings*

# Mexican Custard (Jericalla)

*This custard is light and less rich than that in flan. It is typically heavily spiced with cinnamon sticks, which are baked right with the custard.*

1 quart milk
1 cup sugar
3 or 4 cinnamon sticks
⅛ teaspoon salt
4 eggs
1 teaspoon vanilla extract

1. Combine milk, sugar, and cinnamon sticks in saucepan. Bring to scalding point, stirring constantly. Remove from heat and cool to lukewarm.
2. Meanwhile, beat eggs in a 1½-quart casserole. Gradually beat in milk-sugar mixture; stir in vanilla extract. Place in a shallow pan of water.
3. Bake at 325°F about 1 hour, or until custard is set.
4. Serve warm or cooled.

*About 10 servings*

Refreshing **Sangría, 77,** is often served
with Mexican meals.

# Sherried Raisin-Rice Pudding

⅔ cup raisins
¼ cup sherry
1 cup uncooked rice
1 teaspoon grated lemon peel
Dash salt
1½ cups water
3 cups milk
1 cup sugar
½ teaspoon cinnamon
1 egg, beaten
Whipped cream (optional)

1. Soak raisins in sherry while preparing rest of pudding.
2. Put rice, lemon peel, salt, and water in a saucepan. Bring to boiling, reduce heat, cover, and cook over very low heat until all water is absorbed (about 10 to 15 minutes).
3. Stir in milk, sugar, and cinnamon and cook over very low heat, stirring frequently, until all milk has been absorbed.
4. Stir in soaked raisins, then beaten egg. Continue to heat 1 or 2 minutes, stirring constantly, until egg has cooked.
5. Turn pudding into a serving dish. Chill in refrigerator.
6. Serve with whipped cream, if desired.

*6 to 8 servings*

# Fresh Pineapple and Almond Pudding

*The term "pudding" is somewhat of a misnomer for this dessert, which resembles the luscious English Trifle, but uses readily available and popular Mexican foods—fresh pineapple, almonds, and the inevitable cinnamon flavor.*

2 cups pared diced fresh pineapple
½ cup sugar
½ cup ground blanched almonds
½ cup dry sherry
4 egg yolks, beaten
¼ teaspoon cinnamon
1 dozen ladyfingers, or 12 (4×1-inch) slices sponge or angel food cake
½ cup orange marmalade
½ cup dairy sour cream
1 tablespoon sugar
Toasted slivered almonds

1. Combine pineapple, ½ cup sugar, ground almonds, ¼ cup of the sherry, egg yolks, and cinnamon in a saucepan. Cook over low heat, stirring constantly, until thickened. Cool.
2. Meanwhile, split ladyfingers and spread with marmalade. (If using cake slices, they may be toasted lightly if very soft, but do not split before spreading with marmalade.)
3. Arrange half the spread ladyfingers or cake slices in bottom of a 1½-quart serving dish. Sprinkle with 2 tablespoons sherry. Spoon half the pineapple mixture on top. Repeat layers of ladyfingers, sherry, and pineapple mixture.
4. Set in refrigerator until well chilled (at least 1 hour).
5. Sweeten sour cream with 1 tablespoon sugar. Spread over top of chilled dessert. Decorate with toasted almonds.

*6 to 8 servings*

# Rice with Milk (Arroz con Leche)

*This dessert is similar to rice pudding, but is not as firm. It may be served hot or cold.*

1 cup uncooked rice
1 cup sugar
1 cinnamon stick
1 can (14 ounces) sweetened condensed milk
1 quart milk
1½ teaspoons vanilla extract

1. Put all ingredients into a saucepan; stir. Bring to boiling, then reduce heat to low. Cover and cook until rice is tender, about 2 minutes; stir occasionally to prevent sticking. Remove cinnamon stick.
2. The dessert will be fairly runny. Serve hot or chilled.

*6 to 8 servings*

On January 6, Three Kings' Day, the Christmas season ends with the serving of **Kings' Bread Ring, 93.**

# Viceroy's Dessert (Mexican Trifle)

4 eggs, separated
¾ cup sugar
1 cup milk
1 cup dry sherry
1 teaspoon vanilla extract
Pinch salt
1 cup whipping cream
1 tablespoon confectioners' sugar
2 tablespoons brandy
1 pound sponge cake or ladyfingers
Apricot preserves
Grated semisweet chocolate
Toasted slivered almonds

1. Place egg yolks and sugar in top of a double boiler; beat until evenly mixed, then beat in milk. Place over boiling water and cook until thickened, stirring constantly. Stir in ½ cup of the sherry and vanilla extract. Cool; set aside.

2. Beat egg whites with salt until stiff, not dry, peaks form. Beat cream with confectioners' sugar until stiff; stir in brandy. Fold egg whites into whipped cream mixture. Set aside.

3. Slice sponge cake into ½-inch-thick slices (or split ladyfingers). Spread with apricot preserves.

4. Arrange one layer in 2-quart serving dish (preferably glass, as the finished dessert is pretty). Sprinkle with some of remaining sherry. Spread with a layer of one-third of the custard mixture. Add another layer of cake, sprinkle with sherry, and spread with a third of the cream-egg-white mixture. Repeat layers until all ingredients are used, ending with a layer of cream-egg-white mixture.

5. Sprinkle with chocolate and almonds. Chill in refrigerator several hours.

*6 to 8 servings*

# Almond Snow

2 cups milk
½ cup sugar
¼ cup ground blanched almonds
4 egg whites
Pinch salt
1 tablespoon kirsch
Toasted slivered almonds

1. Scald milk. Stir in sugar until dissolved. Add almonds. Cook over very low heat about 15 minutes. Cool.

2. Meanwhile, beat egg whites with salt until stiff, not dry, peaks form. Fold egg whites into milk mixture. Stir in kirsch.

3. Butter top of a double boiler; pour in mixture; cover. Cook over hot (not boiling) water until mixture is firm. Chill.

4. Unmold onto serving plate and stud with slivered almonds.

*6 servings*

# Sherried Almond Torte

4 eggs, separated
½ cup sugar
1 cup sifted all-purpose flour
1 teaspoon baking powder
¼ teaspoon salt
⅓ cup melted butter or margarine,
    cooled
1 teaspoon vanilla extract
½ teaspoon almond extract
    (optional)
*Sauce and Topping:*
2 cups sugar
2 cups water

1. Beat egg whites until foamy; gradually add 4 tablespoons of the sugar and continue beating until soft peaks form.

2. Beat egg yolks with remaining 4 tablespoons of sugar. Gradually fold beaten yolks into beaten whites.

3. Sift flour, baking powder, and salt together. Sprinkle over egg mixture about ¼ cup at a time and fold in gently. Fold in butter, vanilla extract, and almond extract (if used).

4. Pour into a greased 9-inch square baking pan.

5. Bake at 375°F about 30 minutes, or until golden brown. Remove from oven and pierce all over with a long-handled kitchen fork or ice pick, making holes through to bottom.

6. Meanwhile, prepare sauce. Combine sugar and water in a saucepan and boil over low heat, stirring occasionally, to soft

½ cup sherry
¾ cup toasted slivered almonds

ball stage (234°F). Stir in sherry. Pour hot sauce over hot cake, sprinkling entire top with almonds as last third of sauce is poured over top. Let stand in baking pan until thoroughly cooled. Serve from pan, or remove to a serving plate.

*8 to 10 servings*

# Royal Eggs

*This unusual dessert is typical of those created by the Spanish nuns, who were responsible for a number of the elegant dishes which combined Indian and European ingredients.*

¼ cup raisins
½ cup dry sherry
12 egg yolks
2 cups sugar
1 cup water
1 cinnamon stick
¼ cup slivered almonds

1. Soak raisins in ¼ cup of the sherry.
2. Beat egg yolks until they form a ribbon when poured from the beater.
3. Pour into a buttered shallow pan. Set this pan in another larger pan with about 1 inch of water in it.
4. Bake at 325°F about 20 to 25 minutes, or until set.
5. Remove from oven and cool on a wire rack.
6. Cut cooked, cooled eggs into cubes.
7. Meanwhile, combine sugar, water, and cinnamon stick in a saucepan and bring to boiling. Reduce heat and simmer about 5 minutes, stirring until all sugar is dissolved. Remove cinnamon stick.
8. Carefully place egg cubes in saucepan of sauce. Continue simmering over very low heat until cubes are well-saturated with the syrup. Add soaked raisins and remaining sherry. Sprinkle with slivered almonds.

*6 servings*

# Orange Liqueur Mousse

1 package (3 ounces)
  orange-flavored gelatin
1 cup boiling water
¼ cup cold water
¼ cup orange liqueur
1 cup whipping cream
  Whipped cream (optional)
  Shredded coconut (optional)

1. Dissolve gelatin in boiling water. Add cold water and cool mixture to room temperature. Stir in orange liqueur. Chill in refrigerator until mixture starts to thicken (about 30 minutes).
2. Whip cream until it piles softly. Gradually add gelatin mixture, stirring gently until evenly blended.
3. Pour into a mold. Chill until set.
4. Turn out of mold onto serving plate and top with additional whipped cream and coconut, if desired.

*4 to 6 servings*

# Almendrado

*The colors of the Mexican flag and the Mexican eagle are represented in this red, white, and green layered gelatin dessert served with creamy custard sauce.*

1 tablespoon unflavored gelatin
½ cup sugar
1 cup cold water
4 egg whites
½ teaspoon almond extract
   Red and green food coloring
1 cup finely ground almonds
   Custard Sauce with Almonds

1. Mix gelatin and sugar in a saucepan. Stir in water. Set over low heat and stir until gelatin and sugar are dissolved. Chill until slightly thickened.
2. Beat egg whites until stiff, not dry, peaks are formed. Fold into gelatin mixture along with almond extract. Beat until mixture resembles whipped cream. Divide equally into 3 portions. Color one portion red, another green, and leave the last one white.
3. Pour red mixture into an 8-inch square dish or pan. Sprinkle with half of the almonds. Pour in white mixture and sprinkle with remaining almonds. Top with green layer. Chill thoroughly.
4. Cut into portions and serve with custard sauce.

*12 servings*

**Custard Sauce with Almonds:** Scald **2 cups milk.** Mix **4 egg yolks** and **¼ cup sugar** in the top of a double boiler. Add scalded milk gradually, stirring constantly. Cook over boiling water, stirring constantly until mixture coats a spoon. Remove from water and stir in **¼ teaspoon almond extract** and **½ cup toasted sliced almonds.** Cool; chill thoroughly.

*About 2½ cups*

# Coffee Liqueur Mold

1 envelope unflavored gelatin
¼ cup coffee liqueur
1 cup strong hot coffee
¼ cup sugar
1 cup whipping cream
   Whipped cream (optional)
¼ cup chopped pecans (optional)

1. Soften gelatin in coffee liqueur. Dissolve in hot coffee. Add sugar and stir until dissolved. Cool to lukewarm. Stir in cream.
2. Pour into a mold. Chill until set.
3. To serve, turn out of mold onto serving plate. If desired, top with whipped cream and sprinkle with chopped pecans.

*4 to 6 servings*

# Buñuelos

*Buñuelos are often described as Mexican fritters, but because they are so thin and crisp they're more like a deep-fried cookies. And that's how they are usually served, as a snack or finger dessert. Sometimes they are made small, but are more fun when large.*

4 cups all-purpose flour
2 tablespoons sugar
1 teaspoon baking powder
1 teaspoon salt
2 eggs, well beaten
¾ to 1 cup milk

1. Mix flour with sugar, baking powder, and salt in a bowl.
2. Combine beaten eggs and ¾ cup of the milk. Stir into dry ingredients to make a stiff dough; add more milk if needed to moisten all dry ingredients. Stir in butter.
3. Turn dough onto a lightly floured surface and knead 1 to 2 minutes until smooth. Divide dough into 24 balls. Roll each

¼ cup butter or margarine, melted
Oil for deep frying heated to
    365°F
Granulated sugar-cinnamon
    mixture for dusting

ball into a round about 6 inches in diameter.
4. Fry each round in hot deep fat until delicately browned, turning to fry on second side. Drain on absorbent paper. Sprinkle with sugar-cinnamon mixture while still warm.

*2 dozen buñuelos*

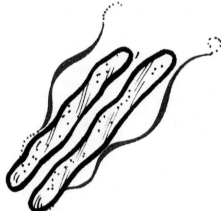

Churros are another deep-fried pastry, a bit sturdier than the delicate buñuelos. Churros are frequently sold by street vendors or at fairs, freshly fried and rolled in sugar. They look somewhat like long twisted strings, from whence comes their name. For they are of Spanish origin, and in Spain a *churro* is a long, coarse-haired sheep with hair that tends to mat into strings—another piece of Mexican food humor. The lime or lemon heated in the frying oil gives churros a distinctive flavor.

## Churros

Oil for deep frying
1 lime or lemon, cut in half
1 cup water
1 tablespoon sugar
1 teaspoon salt
1½ cups all-purpose flour
1 large egg
Granulated sugar

1. Start heating oil in a deep kettle or saucepan; add lime or lemon halves.
2. Put water, sugar, and salt into a saucepan and heat to boiling.
3. Remove from heat and beat in flour until smooth. Add egg and continue to beat until mixture is smooth and satiny.
4. Remove lime pieces from the oil, which should be between 365° and 375°F. Force batter through pastry tube into hot fat. Fry until golden brown.
5. Remove from fat and drain on absorbent paper. Break into 3-inch lengths. Roll in granulated sugar.

*About 1 dozen 3-inch churros*

## Sopaipillas

*Sopaipillas are little pillow-shaped deep-fried pastries. They may be served plain as a bread, or as suggested here, sprinkled with cinnamon-sugar as a dessert. Sometimes they are topped with syrup.*

2 cups sifted all-purpose flour
2 teaspoons baking powder
1 teaspoon salt
2 tablespoons shortening
⅔ to ¾ cup cold water
Oil or shortening for deep frying
    heated to 365°F
Cinnamon sugar

1. Sift flour, baking powder, and salt together into bowl. Cut in shortening until mixture resembles coarse crumbs. Sprinkle water over top and work in gradually until dough will just hold together (as for pie pastry).
2. Turn out on a lightly floured surface and knead gently about 30 seconds. Roll out as thin as possible. Cut into 2-inch squares.
3. Fry one or two at a time in heated fat, turning until puffed and golden brown on both sides.
4. Drain on absorbent paper. Sprinkle with cinnamon sugar while still hot.

*2½ to 3 dozen*

# Empanadas de Dulce

*Empanadas are Mexican-style turnovers, made with a simple pastry. Actually, they are frequently filled with meat, fish, or poultry. But this version is for Empanadas de Dulce—the sweet kind. The pastry has a bit of sugar added. The filling suggestions given are typical of those served for snacks or desserts.*

**Pastry:**
- 2 cups all-purpose flour
- 2 tablespoons sugar
- 2 teaspoons baking powder
- 1 teaspoon salt
- ½ cup lard or shortening
- ⅓ cup ice water (about)

**Fillings:**
- (1) 1 cup chopped pecans
- ¼ cup brown sugar
- 2 tablespoons butter or margarine
- ½ teaspoon cinnamon

- (2) 1 cup drained crushed pineapple
- 2 tablespoons sugar
- ¼ cup flaked coconut

1. Mix flour with sugar, baking powder, and salt in bowl. Cut in lard until mixture resembles coarse crumbs. Sprinkle ice water over flour mixture, stirring lightly with a fork until all dry ingredients hold together.

2. Turn dough onto a lightly floured surface and knead gently 30 seconds. Roll out to a rectangle about 16×12 inches.

3. With a floured knife, cut into twelve 4-inch squares. Place a spoonful of filling in center of each square. Fold one corner over filling to meet opposite corner. Seal by dampening inside edges of pastry and pressing together with tines of fork. Place on a baking sheet.

4. Bake at 400°F 15 to 20 minutes. While still hot, sprinkle tops with **granulated sugar.**

*12 empanadas*

# Mexican-Style French Toast (Torrejas de Coco)

- 1 cup sugar
- ½ cup water
- 1 coconut, drained, shelled, pared, and shredded
- 1 loaf egg bread (1½ pounds), sliced
- 3 eggs
- 1 tablespoon flour
- 1 cup lard
- 3 cups sugar
- 1 cinnamon stick
- 1 cup water
- 3 tablespoons raisins
- ¼ cup chopped blanched almonds or pinenuts

1. Dissolve 1 cup sugar in ½ cup water in a saucepan over medium heat. Bring to boiling; boil 3 minutes. Add shredded coconut; let it cook until the moisture is absorbed and coconut is dry (about 15 minutes). Remove from heat and cool slightly.

2. Put the coconut paste between each two slices of egg bread.

3. Beat eggs with flour; dip both sides of sandwiches in egg and fry in lard in a skillet (about 1 minute on each side). Drain them on absorbent paper.

4. Make a syrup by heating 3 cups sugar, cinnamon, and 1 cup water to boiling in a large skillet; boil 5 minutes. Add browned sandwiches and simmer several minutes; turn once.

5. Arrange desserts on a serving dish, garnish with raisins and almonds, and strain the syrup over all.

*About 12 servings*

# Pecan Cake

- ¾ cup cake flour
- 1 teaspoon baking powder
- 3 eggs, separated
- ⅔ cup sugar
- 1 tablespoon lemon juice

1. Blend flour and baking powder.
2. Beat egg yolks until thick and lemon colored in large bowl of electric mixer. Gradually beat in sugar. Beat in lemon juice and grated pecans, then gradually beat in flour mixture. Slowly beat in melted butter.

½ cup finely grated pecans (use blender or fine knife of vegetable grater to get nuts very fine)

½ cup butter or margarine, melted
  Pinch salt
  Orange Glaze
  Pecan halves for decoration

3. Beat egg whites with salt until stiff peaks form. Fold beaten egg whites into batter.

4. Pour batter into a greased and floured 9-inch round cake pan.

5. Bake at 350°F 30 to 35 minutes, or until cake tester inserted in center comes out clean.

6. Let cake cool 10 minutes before removing from pan. Cool completely on a wire rack, right side up.

7. Place cake on a serving plate and cover with hot orange glaze. Decorate with pecan halves.

*6 to 8 servings*

Orange Glaze: Combine ½ **cup orange marmalade** and ¼ **cup sugar** in a small saucepan and cook until sugar is dissolved (2 to 3 minutes), stirring constantly. Use while still hot.

# Cream-Filled Chestnut Cake

1 pound chestnuts in the shell; or use 1¼ cups pecans, chopped
¾ cup butter
1 cup sugar
½ teaspoon vanilla extract
6 eggs, separated
1¼ cups all-purpose flour
1 teaspoon baking powder
½ cup milk
  Chestnut Cream

1. Prepare chestnuts (see Note).

2. Cream butter with sugar and vanilla extract until fluffy. Mixing well after each addition, add the chestnut purée, then the egg yolks, one at a time.

3. Mix flour with baking powder, and add alternately with milk to the chestnut mixture, mixing well after each addition. Beat egg whites until stiff, but not dry. Fold into batter.

4. Turn mixture into 2 greased and floured 9-inch round layer cake pans.

5. Bake at 350°F about 25 minutes, or until done.

6. Let cool, then put layers together and decorate cake with chestnut cream.

*One 9-inch layer cake*

*Note:* To prepare chestnuts, rinse chestnuts and make a slit on two sides of each shell. Put into a saucepan; cover with boiling water and boil about 20 minutes. Remove shells and skins; return chestnuts to saucepan and cover with boiling salted water. Cover and simmer until chestnuts are tender (10 to 20 minutes). Drain and finely chop.

Chestnut Cream: Prepare ¾ **pound chestnuts** in the shell (see Note above); or use **1 cup pecans**, chopped. Whip **1 cup whipping cream** until thickened. Mix in ⅔ **cup confectioners' sugar** and ½ **teaspoon vanilla extract,** then chestnuts.

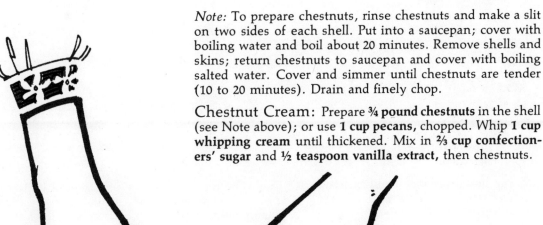

# Anise Cookies

1 package active dry yeast
½ cup warm water
2 teaspoons salt
5 cups all-purpose flour
3 tablespoons sugar
1 cup each butter and vegetable shortening (at room temperature)
4 teaspoons anise extract
1 teaspoon baking powder
Red and green decorating sugar

1. Dissolve yeast in water in a large bowl. Add salt and about 1 cup flour; mix very well. Add all other ingredients except the remaining flour and baking powder; mix thoroughly. Add remaining flour and baking powder; mix well.
2. Make 6 or 8 balls; with the palm of your hand, make long, thin rolls (about the size of the ring finger) and cut them into squares.
3. Place pieces, leaving space between them, on a cookie sheet. Make a cut on top of each.
4. Bake at 350°F about 25 minutes, or until golden brown.
5. Remove from cookie sheet and coat with red and green sugar. Cool on wire racks.

*About 10 dozen*

# Mexican Christmas Cookies (Biscochos)

1 cup vegetable shortening
2 teaspoons grated orange peel
1¼ cups sugar
1 egg
⅓ cup fresh orange juice
3¾ cups all-purpose flour
¼ teaspoon salt
1 teaspoon cinnamon
½ teaspoon ground cloves
½ cup finely chopped pecans
Very fine sugar

1. Cream shortening, orange peel, and sugar until light. Beat in egg, then orange juice.
2. Blend flour, salt, and spices. Stir into creamed mixture. Mix in pecans.
3. Wrap dough and chill overnight.
4. Next day, roll out a small amount at a time on lightly floured surface to ⅛-inch thickness. Cut in desired shapes with fancy cookie cutter.
5. Put on lightly greased cookie sheets.
6. Bake at 375°F 8 to 10 minutes, or until golden brown.
7. Sprinkle with sugar while still warm.

*About 10 dozen*

# Polvorones

*These buttery rich pecan cookies are sometimes called Mexican Wedding Cakes, Bride's Cakes, or simply Polvorones, which Mexicans translate to mean sugar cookies—not because there is much sugar in the dough, but because the warm baked cookies are rolled in confectioners' sugar. Literally the name polvorones means "dusted ones."*

1 cup butter or margarine, softened
1 teaspoon vanilla extract
½ cup confectioners' sugar
2 cups all-purpose flour
¼ teaspoon salt
1 cup finely chopped pecans
Confectioners' sugar

1. Cream butter with vanilla extract until light and fluffy. Add sugar, creaming well. Mix in flour and salt, then pecans.
2. Shape dough into 1-inch balls and flatten slightly. Place on ungreased cookie sheets.
3. Bake at 350°F 25 to 30 minutes, or until lightly browned.
4. Remove from cookie sheets and cool slightly. Roll in confectioners' sugar.

*About 4 dozen cookies*

# Nut Cookies

1 cup butter
¼ cup confectioners' sugar
2 cups all-purpose flour
¾ cup chopped nuts

1. Beat butter until softened. Add sugar and cream well. Add flour and nuts; mix well.
2. Shape into small balls. Place on cookie sheets.
3. Bake at 325°F 15 to 20 minutes.
4. While still warm, coat with **confectioners' sugar.**

*About 5½ dozen cookies*

# Apricot-Filled Pastries *(Pastelitos)*

1 cup dried apricots
1 cup water
½ cup sugar
½ teaspoon vanilla extract
2 cups all-purpose flour
¾ teaspoon salt
½ teaspoon baking powder
⅔ cup lard
4 to 6 tablespoons icy cold water
Confectioners' Sugar Glaze

1. Put apricots and water into saucepan. Cover, bring to boiling, and cook 20 minutes.
2. Turn contents of saucepan into an electric blender; cover and blend until smooth.
3. Combine blended apricots and sugar in saucepan; cook until thick (about 5 minutes). Cool slightly; stir in vanilla extract.
4. Mix flour, salt, and baking powder in a bowl. Cut in lard until crumbly. Add cold water, 1 tablespoon at a time, tossing with a fork until dough holds together. Divide in half.
5. Roll each half of dough to a 14×10-inch rectangle on a lightly floured surface.
6. Line a 13×9×2-inch baking pan with one rectangle of dough. Spread apricot mixture evenly over dough. Place remaining dough on top; seal edges. Prick top crust.
7. Bake at 400°F 25 minutes, or until lightly browned around edges.
8. Cool slightly. Frost with confectioners' sugar glaze. Cool; cut in squares.

*2 dozen filled pastries*

Confectioners' Sugar Glaze: Combine **1 cup confectioners' sugar** and ½ teaspoon vanilla extract. Blend in **milk or cream** (about 3 tablespoons) until glaze is of spreading consistency.

Ice cream topped with tropical fruit seems a perfect dessert for spicy Mexican food. Here are two such suggestions for fruit and ice desserts with a Mexican accent. In both cases the fruit with its flaming sauce can be served alone, if preferred.

# Flaming Bananas

2 tablespoons butter or margarine
⅔ cup sugar
6 ripe bananas, peeled
½ cup rum

1. Melt butter in a chafing dish or skillet. Stir in sugar and heat until sugar melts.
2. Slice bananas lengthwise and add to butter-sugar mixture; turn to coat on all sides. Pour in rum and keep over medium heat.
3. Flame sauce by pouring a little rum into a teaspoon and holding it over flame of chafing dish or range until it flames; then use this flaming rum to light rum on top of bananas. Spoon flaming sauce over fruit several times.
4. Serve over **vanilla or chocolate ice cream.**

*6 servings*

# Flaming Mangos

2 fresh mangos, or 12 slices canned
   mango, about ½ inch thick
1 cup orange juice
2 tablespoons sugar
1 cup tequila

1. Wash and peel fresh mangos; cut each into 6 slices. Place in chafing dish or skillet. Pour orange juice over fruit and sprinkle with sugar. Heat to simmering, stirring gently to dissolve sugar and coat fruit. After 3 or 4 minutes, pour in tequila; keep over medium heat.
2. Flame sauce by pouring a little tequila into teaspoon and holding it over flame of chafing dish or range until it flames; then use this flaming tequila to light tequila on top of mangos.
3. Serve over **vanilla ice cream.**

*6 servings*

Caramel—called "cajeta" in Mexico—is a popular flavor for both candy and ice cream. Mexican cajeta is a much more delicate flavor than our North American caramel, and well worth the eating. The flavor name, which literally means "little box," came about in an unusual way. On Sundays and holidays, at fiestas and fairs or wherever a crowd in holiday mood is likely to pass by, street vendors (usually small children) stand where the traffic is heaviest selling little round or oval-shaped wooden boxes (cajetas) filled with a very soft caramel candy; each little box is accompanied by a tiny spoon with which the candy is eaten directly from the box. The candy became so popular that its true and probably more descriptive name, "dulce de leche" or milk candy, gradually was changed to "cajeta" because of the containers in which it is sold. Following is an old-fashioned recipe for making this delicious candy. You may wish to eat it with a spoon, pour it over ice cream, sandwich it between two cookies, or serve it as a sauce over plain cake. Because the original method for making cajeta requires several hours of slow cooking, a second recipe follows for producing cajeta with a short-cut method.

# Caramel Candy *(Cajeta)*

**2 quarts milk**
**3 cups sugar**
**¼ teaspoon baking soda**
**1 cinnamon stick (optional)**
**1 teaspoon vanilla extract**

1. Combine 1 quart of the milk and the sugar in a saucepan. Cook over very low heat until golden in color, stirring occasionally (this may take 2 to 3 hours).
2. Place second quart of milk in separate saucepan; add baking soda and cinnamon stick (if used). Bring to boiling; remove from heat and discard cinnamon stick. Add hot milk to caramelized milk-sugar mixture very gradually, stirring constantly. Cook over very low heat until thick, stirring occasionally (another hour of cooking may be needed).
3. Cool and stir in vanilla extract. Pour into a serving bowl or several individual cups.

*About 1 quart candy*

**Cajeta from Condensed Milk:** Place unopened cans of **sweetened condensed milk** in a deep kettle. Cover completely with water. Simmer, uncovered, 3 hours. As water starts to evaporate below tops of cans, add **boiling water** to keep tops well covered. Remove cans from water and cool. Open cans and spoon candied milk into serving dish. Chill.

**Cajeta (Pressure Cooker Method):** This is an even faster method of achieving candy from sweetened condensed milk. Place unopened cans of milk in pressure cooker. Pour in water to about half the depth of cans. Cover cooker and cook under pressure for 45 minutes. Reduce pressure gradually. Cool. Open cans and pour into serving dish. Chill.

*Note:* If desired, candy made by either of these methods can be flavored with sherry or other wine. Pour **1 can candy** into saucepan and add **¼ cup wine.** Cook and stir over low heat until wine is absorbed. Cool; pour into serving dish. Chill.

# Christmas Candy Balls

**2 medium potatoes, scrubbed (do not pare)**
**1 cup sugar**
**1 teaspoon vanilla extract**
**2 cups chopped pecans**
**1 cup confectioners' sugar**
**1 teaspoon ground cinnamon**
    **Candied red or green cherries, cut in halves**

1. Cook potatoes in their skins, peel, press through ricer or food mill. Mix in sugar, vanilla extract, and nuts. Chill.
2. Form little balls; coat them with confectioners' sugar mixed with cinnamon. Put into small fluted paper cups and garnish with cherry halves.
3. Store in refrigerator until ready to serve.

*About 2 dozen balls*

# Pinenut Balls

1 pound pinenuts
1 cup sweetened condensed milk
3 cups confectioners' sugar
   Confectioners' sugar to coat

1. Grind pinenuts and mix with sweetened condensed milk and confectioners' sugar.
2. Shape into 1-inch balls and coat them with sugar. Put onto a waxed paper lined tray. Let stand until set.

*About 6 dozen*

# Orange Candy

3 cups sugar
¼ cup water
1 cup undiluted evaporated milk
   Pinch salt
2 teaspoons grated orange peel
1 cup chopped walnuts

1. Put 1 cup sugar into a heavy, light-colored skillet and stir over medium heat with a wooden spoon until sugar is melted and caramelized (cooked to a golden brown color). Add water and stir until sugar is completely dissolved.
2. Add remaining sugar, milk, and salt. Cook over low heat, stirring until mixture begins to boil. Cook, stirring frequently, to 230°F on candy thermometer (soft-ball stage).
3. Remove from heat. Cool to lukewarm; do not stir.
4. Meanwhile, lightly butter an 8-inch square pan.
5. Add grated peel and nuts to lukewarm mixture. Beat until candy loses gloss and holds its shape when dropped from a spoon.
6. Press into buttered pan and cool. Cut into small squares.

*About 1½ pounds*

# Mexican Molasses Candy

1 cup light molasses
1 cup firmly packed brown sugar
2 tablespoons butter or margarine
1 teaspoon cider vinegar
¾ teaspoon almond extract
1½ cups toasted slivered almonds

1. Put molasses, brown sugar, butter, and vinegar into a heavy saucepan. Bring to boiling. Boil hard about 7 to 12 minutes, until mixture reaches 260°F on a candy thermometer (firm ball stage).
2. Remove from heat and add almond extract and almonds; stir.
3. Pour onto a greased baking sheet, spread as thin as possible, and cool. Break into 2-inch pieces.

*About 1 pound*

The Christmas season in Mexico is very festive, and the time of celebration lasts through January 6, dubbed Three Kings' Day (Epiphany or Twelfth Night). This is a traditional gift-giving day, especially for the children. As is so often true of special religious holidays throughout the world, a traditional rich, fruit-filled yeast bread is baked and served for Three Kings' Day. This special bread, called Rosca de Reyes (Kings' Bread Ring) has an added touch—a small china doll baked into the bread. Whoever gets the piece of bread with the doll is expected to play host for a Candlemas Day party on February 2.

# Kings' Bread Ring *(Rosca de Reyes)*

2 packages active dry yeast or 2
    cakes compressed yeast
½ cup water water (hot for dry
    yeast, lukewarm for
    compressed)
½ cup milk, scalded
⅓ cup sugar
⅓ cup shortening
2 teaspoons salt
4 cups all-purpose flour (about)
3 eggs, well beaten
2 cups chopped candied fruits
    (citron, cherries, and orange
    peel)
Melted butter or margarine
Confectioners' Sugar Icing

1. Soften yeast in water.
2. Pour hot milk over sugar, shortening, and salt in large bowl, stirring until sugar is dissolved and shortening melted. Cool to lukewarm. Beat in 1 cup of the flour, then eggs and softened yeast. Add enough more flour to make a stiff dough. Stir in 1½ cups candied fruits, reserving remainder to decorate baked ring.
3. Turn dough onto a floured surface and knead until smooth and satiny. Roll dough under hands into a long rope; shape into a ring, sealing ends together. Transfer to a greased cookie sheet. Push a tiny china doll into dough so it is completely covered. Brush with melted butter.
4. Cover with a towel and let rise in a warm place until double in bulk (about 1½ hours).
5. Bake at 375°F 25 to 30 minutes, or until golden brown.
6. Cool on wire rack. Frost with Confectioners' Sugar Icing and decorate with reserved candied fruit.

*1 large bread ring*

*Confectioners' Sugar Icing:* Blend 1⅓ cups confectioners' sugar, 4 teaspoons water, and ½ teaspoon vanilla extract.

# Sweet Rolls *(Molletes)*

2 packages active dry yeast
½ cup warm water
½ cup sugar
½ teaspoon salt
1 tablespoon anise seed
½ cup butter or margarine, melted
3 eggs, at room temperature
3¾ to 4¾ cups all-purpose flour
1 egg yolk
2 tablespoons light corn syrup

1. Sprinkle yeast over water in a large warm bowl. Stir until yeast is dissolved. Add sugar, salt, anise seed, melted butter, eggs, and 2 cups of flour; beat until smooth. Stir in enough additional flour to make a soft dough.
2. Turn dough onto a lightly floured surface; knead until smooth and elastic (8 to 10 minutes).
3. Put dough into a greased bowl; turn to grease top. Cover; let rise in a warm place until double in bulk (about 1 hour).
4. Punch dough down and turn onto lightly floured surface; roll into a 12-inch square. Cut into fourths and cut each square into 4 triangles.
5. Allowing space for rising, place triangles on greased cookie sheets. Cover; let rise in warm place until double in bulk (about 1 hour).
6. Beat egg yolk and corn syrup together until blended. Generously brush over triangles.
7. Bake at 350°F 10 to 15 minutes. Serve warm.

*16 large rolls*

# INDEX

# Culinary Arts Institute

## Adventures in Cooking SERIES

This series of cookbooks is designed to bring adventure and variety to the tables of American families everywhere. Good eating is the premise of these easy-on-the-cook recipes, which follow the simple, self-explanatory style made famous by the Culinary Arts Institute. Each book has 96 pages of recipes, menus, and how-to instructions, plus 8 pages of full-color photographs. Each book is fully indexed, and measures 7¹³⁄₁₆" x 10¼". Softcover. Retail price: $1.95 each.

### ORDER YOUR COPIES TODAY

# Culinary Arts Institute

## THE OUTDOOR COOKBOOK
Everything you need to know about cooking outdoors using all kinds of equipment. Includes food preparation and packing for outings, easy-on-the-cook backyard feasts, fire-building tips, cooking afloat, and, of course, kitchen-tested recipes for every conceivable kind of dish from appetizers to desserts.

## THE CANNING AND FREEZING BOOK
Basic techniques for preparing, canning, and freezing every kind of food, with many, many how-to drawings and kitchen-tested recipes. Fashion your own "TV dinners" from your family's favorite recipes; buy bargains when you find them—serve them when you need them.

## WINE IN COOKING AND DINING
Sets you at ease with wines, explaining how and when to serve them and how to use them in food to best advantage. Maps and diagrams, how-to drawings, and several chapters of kitchen-tested recipes calling for wine.

## THE BUDGET COOKBOOK
Budgets don't have to mean dull meals, and this book has many chapters of kitchen-tested recipes which prove it. Helps you plan, shop, store, and cook economically, yet no one will suspect they're being served a "budget meal."

## PARTIES FOR ALL SEASONS
Kitchen-tested recipes, entertaining ideas, serving suggestions, menus and more, for a full year of holidays, special events, and non-events. Includes children's parties, family occasions, teen-age bashes, strictly grown-up affairs, bachelor brunches, picnics, and others.

## CROCKERY COOKING
The slow pot is fast becoming a favorite in busy households, and this book tells how to use it to best advantage for all kinds of dishes including appetizers, soups, breads, main dishes, and desserts with a surprising array of kitchen-tested recipes.

## POLISH COOKBOOK
Traditional Polish foods, with recipes tested and proven for American kitchens, using ingredients available at most supermarkets. Also includes history of and interesting facts about Polish food, how to prepare a Polish feast, and other fascinating information to guide Polish and non-Polish cooks alike.

## BREAD AND SOUP COOKBOOK
Two staples of the American diet are combined here for good eating on all occasions, including breakfast, lunch, dinner, supper, and snacks. The emphasis is on nutrition and the pleasure of eating, an unbeatable combination in itself.

## MEXICAN COOKBOOK
Authentic Mexican dishes styled for preparation in American kitchens, with special emphasis on finding Mexican ingredients or making proper substitutions. Corn, beans, and chilies are the Mexican staples, but there is much more here.

## ITALIAN COOKBOOK
Elegant gourmet dishes or hearty peasant fare—it's all here the way you want to taste it. Kitchen-tested recipes styled for American cooks. You can even make your own pasta. This is the ideal book for beginners or experienced cooks alike.

## THE COOKIE JAR
Cookies from around the world, kitchen-tested for your own home preparation. Recipes for filled, dropped, refrigerated, molded, pressed, and cut cookies; many how-to drawings.

# Adventures in Cooking Cookbooks

*Order your copies now or see your local retail outlet.*

## only $1.95 each

TO ORDER... indicate on the order form the quantity of each book you want @ $1.95 each. Carefully total the amount of the order and add 5% sales tax if you are an Illinois resident. Print your name and address on the shipping label; fold the envelope; enclose your check or money order for the full amount due; seal the envelope, stamp, and mail. Allow 6 weeks for delivery.

## ORDER FORM

Culinary Arts Institute, P.O. Box 7770-A, Chicago, Illinois 60680

Please send me postpaid the Adventures in Cooking cookbooks indicated below, @ $1.95 ea.

| QUANTITY | TITLE | PRICE |
|---|---|---|
| _____ | The Outdoor Cookbook | _____ |
| _____ | The Canning and Freezing Book | _____ |
| _____ | Wine in Cooking and Dining | _____ |
| _____ | The Budget Cookbook | _____ |
| _____ | Parties for All Seasons | _____ |
| _____ | Crockery Cooking (available April, 1976) | _____ |
| _____ | Polish Cookbook (available May, 1976) | _____ |
| _____ | Bread and Soup Cookbook (available June, 1976) | _____ |
| _____ | Mexican Cookbook (available August, 1976) | _____ |
| _____ | Italian Cookbook (available October, 1976) | _____ |
| _____ | The Cookie Jar (available November, 1976) | _____ |
| | Illinois residents add 5% sales tax | _____ |
| | TOTAL CHARGE | _____ |

*I am enclosing* ☐ *check* ☐ *money order (no stamps, please)*

**PRINT YOUR NAME AND ADDRESS HERE — THIS WILL BE USED AS THE SHIPPING LABEL**

Name_____

Address_____

City_____ State_____ Zip_____

Culinary Arts Institute
P.O. Box 7770-A
Chicago, Illinois 60680

THEN FOLD HERE

FIRST FOLD HERE

FOLD HERE LAST

FINALLY, FOLD HERE AND SEAL

DETACH CAREFULLY BEFORE FOLDING TO MAIL